THE CRAFT
OF WRITING

THE CRAFT
OF WRITING

WILLIAM SLOANE

EDITED BY JULIA H. SLOANE

W. W. NORTON & COMPANY NEW YORK

Library of Congress Cataloging in Publication Data
Sloane, William Milligan, 1906–
The craft of writing.

1. Fiction—Authorship. I. Sloane, Julia H.
II. Title.
PN3355.S56 808.3 78-24551
ISBN 0-393-04471-8

2 3 4 5 6 7 8 9 0

CONTENTS

6

CONTENTS

INTRODUCTION

In 1940, as trade manager of then Henry Holt & Co., a trim young man named William Sloane, who looked like the president of some recent Princeton graduating class, published my first book of poems in an act of editorial benevolence I then believed to be no more than my due. Fifteen years later, the same William Sloane, as director of Rutgers University Press, and looking like the president of a less recent Princeton graduating class, published my *As If, Poems New and Selected*. At lunch just before the latter publication, Sloane was jovial but wry.

"In 1940," he began, forming his words around the stem of his pipe, "I squandered a modest but accountable sum of Henry Holt's money on a first book by a lean and hungry young poet. From the meager resources of the University Press, I am about to squander a second sum to publish the selected poems of a not-so-young, not-so-lean, but probably still hungry poet. In an effort to justify this extravagance, I have read the manuscript and in it I discover that not one of those first poems on which I squandered Henry Holt's money struck that poet as good enough to be included in the selected poems."

Bill liked preambles. He finished this one, fussed with his pipe, got it going, and moved to his point. "How," he said, "am I to justify my handling of the money once entrusted to me by Henry Holt? How am I to justify my present handling of the Press's funds? And what sort of an editor does that make me?"

"Let me start," I said, "by suggesting the word 'genius.' You are the sort of editor who can recognize talent even when it isn't there."

Over the years, Bill liked to return to this bit of banter in which he ruefully confessed his gullibility while implying my sly entrapment of his good nature. Yet, even in play, he was touching a serious side of himself. I was moved to dismiss that first book as juvenilia and to sweep those poems under the carpet. Bill was forever moved to ask himself what he had done, why he had done it, and if he had done it well enough. I have never known a man so dedicated to the idea of giving a consistent shape and purpose to his life.

It was never a case of being prostrate before his own image. It was a modest thing, almost, I felt, a sense of curatorship, of discharging his debt to many good men from whose example he had shaped his own sense of purpose. Bill sought to give shape to his life as a novelist gives shape to his book, which is to say in answer to some ideal sense of form.

Since he was an editor, he meant to be the best possible editor. He had a long series of outstanding editorial successes. When he established the publishing firm of William

Introduction

Sloane Associates, there was every indication of a nova in New York publishing. Bill loved the excitement of running his own firm. He brought out a brilliant list of books, and plunged into his new career with confidence. One year for his birthday at Bread Loaf we all gave him silly presents with rhyming sentiments. The rhyme with my gift read:

> Nothing ever nauseates
> The William Sloane Associates.

He swore to make it part of his logo. Someone must have persuaded him to hold back, but for the next few years that motto was prominently displayed in his office.

Those were expansive years. Then bit by bit Bill found he had overextended himself financially. His editorial genius kept pulling rabbits out of hats but it was not enough to hold off his creditors. When he lost control of his firm it must have been like losing his own name. Yet I never heard him lament. He took his losses, analyzing the reasons for them as one might take bearings on a long journey, satisfied himself that he knew what had happened and where he was, and then he simply moved on to the next thing.

When, after a short, unhappy interval with Funk & Wagnalls, he moved to Rutgers and took modest office as the director of the University Press, he simply set out to be as good as he could possibly be at that job. Whatever one does, he believed, must be done as part of an examined life. And reported to his own sense of those mentors who had been most important to him. Some failure is part of man's lot, but a well-lived life must keep its direction.

He was only half serious in twitting me about his shamefaced role in my first book. He was far more serious about having rejected the manuscript of *Look Homeward Angel*. That was a story he returned to many times over the years.

That manuscript had arrived in a crate. Its handwritten pages, he liked to say, would have stacked two feet higher than a grand piano and he had read from the top of the stack to the keyboard—something over 200,000 words—before rejecting it for publication.

When, later, the book, as edited by Max Perkins, was published and scored a great success, Bill had to ask himself in what way he had failed. He read the published book and found in it not one word of the 200,000 he had read. Where in that crate of manuscript had Max Perkins found the book he published?

Perkins, as it turned out, had worked under special imperatives. He had owed Wolfe's agent a favor and the agent had made him promise that he would read to the end before making up his mind. From somewhere in the late pages of that random and endless manuscript Perkins had assembled the book we know. In fact, the title page should have read: "written by Thomas Wolfe, given form by Maxwell Perkins."

Yet I cannot believe that such knowledge was much solace to Bill. He could acknowledge that staying with it through a sampling of 200,000 words was a better than average effort. Yet it had not been the best possible editorial decision. He had, indeed, failed, and he had to search within himself for the reasons for that failure. He had to test himself against that knowledge of failure.

Let me try a guess at the reasons for that decision.

I have never known a man with a more acute sense of what makes a book readable. Readability, I have been told, is not everything. Neither is breathing, but it does come before whatever comes next. Bill knew the difference between the readability of popular fiction (his own two novels are received classics of the science fiction fen) and the readability of, say, Melville and Mann.

It was, I suspect, Wolfe's damnable *unreadability* that finally moved Bill to ship back that crate of manuscript. Edward Dahlberg used to have a favorite tirade in which he denounced Wolfe as "the spermless leviathan—all that bulk and no spark." Dahlberg of course, was out for a verbal flourish. Yet his point is there to be made. Except at his best moments Wolfe remains our least readable important writer. Diffuse his natural randomness through thousands of pages of unrevised and unedited manuscript and only an editor under the compulsion of a promise given could have trudged on far enough to find the salvageable Wolfe.

If it was Bill's insistence on readability that turned him away from Wolfe, that same insistence made him an ideal editor of thousands of other manuscripts. I have never known a man who was more learned and more lucid in discussing the structure of fiction and nonfiction, the management of a scene, or the contract of art and craft that binds reader to author and author to reader in the shared experience of the writing.

To discuss method is to imply rules. Many of today's authors will dismiss any such implication as absurd, insisting that only "the flow of soul" matters. But to dismiss this book on such grounds (themselves, as I believe, absurd) is to ignore what it says.

It offers no inviolable rules. Rather, a deeply read and sensitive editor has studied the practice of past masters and extracted from that practice what he took to be the enduring principles of the art.

Within a single scene, for example, it seems to be unwise to have access to the inner reflections of more than one character. The reader generally needs a single character as the means of perception, as the character to whom the events are happening, as the character with whom he is to empathize in order to have the events of the writing happen to him.

Bill never implied that there are fixed limits to the art and craft of writing. He recognized that what we call the avant-garde (where is it today?) is made up of those who push at practiced limits. Yet, he insisted that even the most experimental writer must be aware of thousands of points-of-craft as general rules of thumb, which can be safely violated only by those who know that such general rules have been legislated into being by the past masters. The particulars Bill here develops into his critical theory are what sound fingering is to a pianist: to learn fingering does not make a concert artist, but no one becomes a concert artist without having learned it.

This book is about the theory and craft of the writer. It recognizes the *je ne sais quoi* that can at times flare to mad splendor. But how does one write about the mysteries of genius? Bill has written the book of what it is possible to say. It is a useful book. In the course of being useful, it re-

Introduction

leases the aura of one good man's mind, whereby the aura around the saying—as always happens in the best writing— becomes even more useful than the thing said.

Bill is dead now. Yet I keep turning corners in my psyche and bumping into him for long conversations. When, in one such encounter, I told him I was writing this introduction he looked wary until I assured him that I was going to call it "the book by the almost best possible editor." He understood that I was apologizing for being one—the lesser—of the two mistakes I had known him to make with a publisher's money.

If there is a third to be made it will be the reader's failure to read what this good man has to say.

John Ciardi
Metuchen, N.J.

EDITOR'S NOTE

For some years before he died, my husband intended "to write a book about how to write a book." He had gone so far as to make a list of chapter headings, and had, in his own words, "sat down at the magic keyboard and hammered out some pages for a preliminary chapter."

With those pages as a beginning, what follows has been selected from folders whose rusted paper clips held twenty years of lecture notes and outlines. But the content is not rusted. William Sloane's convictions about writing as a craft, though expressed with more assurance as the years went by, were the same in 1971 as in 1951.

Selecting the material that would best carry out his intent, and fitting it together, was like assembling a jigsaw puzzle. First, to form the frame, the straight-edged pieces had to be found and interlocked. Then, one had to gather together all the bits that looked like stained-glass windows, and those that surely must be sky and clouds. There a face and shoulder. Here an arm and hand. And so on. The result is only a token of the book my husband would have written, but it is his words and his tone of voice.

EDITOR'S NOTE

My thanks go to the writers who sent me his letters, and my special gratitude to Carol Houck Smith, who knows about assembling puzzles, and to Eric Swenson who said, "There's a book here without anybody adding a mumbling word."

Julia H. Sloane
October, 1978

THE CRAFT
OF WRITING

One

PRELIMINARY

Lord knows, this is not the first book on writing and the writer. There appear to be thousands of them, even if you leave out the accounts by writers themselves of how they wrote what they wrote. The number of titles currently in print and offered for sale certainly runs into the many hundreds; magazines devoted to the problems of writers go out at a rate that is certainly not less than 100,000 copies a month and probably the figure is a good deal higher. Unless he has no mail address at all, the writer in the modern world is not cut off from communion with his kind. All told, the combined instruction and encouragement thus afforded the part-time or beginning writer is more than sufficient to subtract seriously from the time he ought to be devoting to more important reading.

Today's writers of all kinds and ages are also endowed

with another kind of opportunity—the home study course. There are plenty of these, and with prices to fit almost every pocket. Some are university extension courses. Others are profit ventures. In a good many cases they are conducted by qualified and competent people. I myself once enrolled in such a course, given long ago by Columbia, and the experience was of great unintentional value. After some weeks of correspondence with an excellent teacher I discovered that what I was trying to write as a play was really a novel. It was a lesson I have never forgotten because the novel turned out to be a modest success, and from that day to this many better dramatists than I shall ever be have tried unsuccessfully to make a play or a motion picture out of it. Put concisely, the lesson was to let the material dictate the form.

Home study courses seem to work for some people. The proprietors of the nonacademic ones almost always cite success stories from present or former enrollees in their promotion matter. These people, and they are very real people indeed, have written things that sold to publications and have received checks for their writing. More than that, they have seen themselves in print, as some of them express the matter, and found an outlet for their need to achieve an individual identification in a mass-organized world.

Every year in the United States several dozen writers' conferences offer beginning writers a chance to learn, and established writers a chance to teach. The members of these conferences often profit as much from each other as from the staff lectures and workshops, and the companionship of like-minded people, in limited doses, can prove stimulating. The very fact that writing is one of the least gregarious of

occupations makes occasional attendance at a writing conference pleasurable and to some extent instructive.

At least, I am compelled to think so. I have been on the
staff of the oldest of the conferences, the one at Bread Loaf,
Vermont, on the summer, mountain campus of Middlebury
College, for a quarter of a century. In those many years I
have seen a large number of professional writers with whom
I had no other professional connection at close range. From
two or three I learned more than from any men and women
I have even known outside my father, my wife, three of my
teachers, and my professional colleagues. Most of them are
now dead, but they flourished in one of the great periods of
American writing and were a part of it. Bernard De Voto,
Fletcher Pratt, Edith Mirrielees, John Ciardi, Robert Frost,
Louis Untermeyer, Wallace Stegner, Catherine Drinker
Bowen—these are the names of vivid, intensely alive, uncon-
trollably imaginative people with a common passion for
writing and an affection for the people who write or try to
write.

Yet, on balance I believe that for me the greatest single
part of the experience was the dealing, each year, with ten
or a dozen unsuccessful writers, people with troubles that
they had not been able to solve for themselves or with the
advice of their teachers and their families. As the years went
on I began to notice that these writers were, by my stan-
dards, far from hopeless cases. There were a good many of
those, certainly, and an even larger number who really pre-
ferred to dog-paddle rather than swim, but the rest—and it
runs, I think, to a thumping ten percent, of all of them—
went away, revised, worked on their books with their eyes

open, and got published in fairly short order. Any editor will tell you that nowhere near ten percent of his manuscripts are salvageable within the editorial office and process.

So, there is virtue also in the writers' conference.

Then why, with all the books, magazines, schools, courses, and conferences, undertake to expose nonarrived writers to yet another piece of instruction? Why add another book to the mile-long shelf? The only honest answer to these questions is that to do so may, indeed, be a mistake, and an arrogant one at that. But experience has taught me that no two writers are alike, each needs to be worked with, and for, in a different way. This particular book has not been previously written by anyone else; perhaps it will make sense to some of its readers because it attempts to say some familiar truths in a different way. If it does that for only a handful of writers it will have discharged its duty and served its purpose.

The relationship in writing is a one-to-one relationship. There is the writer and there is the reader. One of each. At any given instant there may be any number of such paired relationships going on, but that is an enumerative fact, not a psychological one.

And that brings us to the editor. What is he and what does he do? He is a reader, perhaps the author's first real reader. The editor is a specialist about reading. His specialty is what is sufficiently general and common between a possible readership and what the author has to say. The tool he works with is himself. If the author cannot reach him, he can't reach the editor's readership either. That is the assumption. The editor is much more actively creative than the ordinary reader. He is not correcting themes or marking off for spelling. He is listening for the sound of people in what the author has submitted. He judges character by whether readers will recognize and believe. He judges dialogue by whether readers will hear it. And so on.

This does not mean literalism or realism of treatment. The editor knows that people also dream and sing and pray and hurt inside themselves and to themselves. He also knows that people will pretend, will make-believe, will go seek the hidden and not step on cracks because of their mother's backs, and invent dreamworlds, and play myriad games. He knows that the writer will find people to play his game if he makes the game a real game.

Editors also know that the people who are really readers want to read. They hunger to read. They will forgive a vast number of clumsinesses and scamped work of every sort if the author will delight them just enough to keep them able to continue.

My entire professional life has been spent as an editor, publisher, and writer, with teaching as its major public avocation. The professional editor and the teacher of writing are farther apart than is generally realized. The editor often works with accepted material or with accepted authors, and he works by definition with writers who have arrived—at least to the extent of a check or a publishing contract. The teacher works with beginners who have not yet reached the graduate world of the editor. Both at Bread Loaf and at Rutgers, where I sometimes teach an undergraduate course, I necessarily confront writing that is assigned to me, not writing that I selected for publishable merit, as was the case in the years I spent as a New York book publisher and editor.

The serious teacher of writing quickly discovers that he cannot edit, in the professional sense, the material that is turned in to him. It is not even a question of trying to make a silk purse out of a sow's ear—there is generally neither pig nor poke, no animal and no silk worms. The teacher is compelled, most of the time, to resort to principles, and when he describes them he is little better off because his pupil does not know how to apply them. Indeed, the pupil-writer frequently maintains that principles are the death of creativity in general and his own in particular. Class or workshop sessions at which a piece of writing is read aloud and discussed by the members as a group have, it seems to me, only one merit. They constitute a kind of clumsy publication, a specialized but still public exposure of the writing to other minds.

The drawbacks are numerous. Writing is meant to be read, not read aloud—at least nowadays. In reading aloud, the mere time required for the exposure of the piece is several times that of reading to one's self, and alters the apparent size of the work. It enters the mind of its public through the ear instead of the eye, posing a number of complicated psychological questions in so doing. The reaction of the audience is public, not private as is a reader's. The group to which the story or article is read is an audience, and a reader is not an audience, no matter how many times he is multiplied. Audiences generate a group experience familiar to every actor; writing is meant to induce a private experience in the reader.

Preliminary

So the most successful teachers of writing rely heavily upon individual conferences with the writers in the class, one at a time. This is the way in which a good editor works with the authors in his charge. It is also the way in which all authors, and particularly beginning ones, want to be worked with. It would be a mistake to suppose that the motivation is purely egocentric—a natural expression of the author's belief in his own specialness. It may be that, but it is never entirely that.

The experience at a well-run writers' conference is no different. No matter how brilliant the lectures or how lively the workshop sessions may be, the conferees almost live for the hour of their appointment with the staff member. Many of them come to such interviews with a long list of questions, highly particularized, to which they want answers, very specific answers. The dialogue might go something like this:

"Is this scene where Joe tells Sally that their life together has been a mistake done too obliquely?"

"Let's see . . . that's about page 245. I am worried that the reader will not get that far. Let's talk for a minute about the opening pages."

"Oh, I'm going to write those over. Tell me, does the character of Arthur seem exaggerated to you?"

"Arthur's the father's cousin, isn't he? Well, he didn't seem to have much to do with the rest of the novel. You gave him some good lines, though."

"Everybody in my family liked Arthur. A lot of them think I got him from my Uncle Dick." A pause. "Do you think the manuscript is ready for submission yet?"

"Let's talk about that later."

"If you prefer. Now let's see . . . oh, I wondered about the black boy. Jim. Do you think anyone will take offense at the way I've drawn him?"

And so it goes. But these interviews demonstrate over and over again the vacuum in which the beginning or the unsuccessful writer works. It is a vacuum less social than the writer thinks, and more professional than he wants to believe. The questions he brings to the interview are human enough, but they are often naïve and generally shallow by contrast with the troubles of the manuscript itself. Since a writers' conference or a semester course have termination dates, the writer is being graduated into a world in which he will have to be his own teacher, his own staff member, and his own editor, until he arrives and is published.

If this book has usefulness, that is what it can perhaps provide—a simplified professional way of approaching the process of writing that will save time, improve revision, and enable its readers to come somewhat closer to saying what they want to say, in words, and on paper.

In the pages to follow there will be almost nothing about writing as an art. Art is always a *result,* in any field, whether writing or painting or music, and it is indefinable. Certainly it is not an element of anything that is written, but one effect of what has been written. All great artists appear to be masters of their technique, and masters of that technique in their individual idiom. If the idiom is sufficiently individual, and the technique sufficiently persuasive, many other people are moved to participate in the artist's experience. But this is clearly all a matter of result. Art cannot be taught. No more can the greatness that it conveys.

What *can* be taught is technique, craft, method, understanding of the medium. Any writer or would-be writer would be well advised to reflect that a mastery of craft is just exactly that and has nothing to do with greatness or power except to enhance it. Some important writers have been miserable craftsmen—Henry Miller and Theodore Dreiser to mention two out of our own time. Their books have power and weight and—the combination of those two attributes—impact. My contention here is only that bad writing of the Miller or the Dreiser kind—without the sheer mass energy behind that bad writing—is bad writing and nothing more. Without that power, neither of those two writers would be worth reading. Had they possessed a technique somewhat less like a rockslide, their books would have been better books, and more certain of permanence. The craft of writing serves the art of writing and sharpens it.

Craftsmanship is the use of tools and materials in order to make something in a seemly and economical fashion. For instance, it is *not* craftsmanship to decide to build a table and buy half the lumberyard and have, when the table is finished, approximately eighty or ninety oddly shaped pieces of wood lying around on the floor and hundreds of bent nails and screws and great piles of sawdust. Craftsmanship does indeed carry with it this element of economy of materials. And when it is appropriate to the object being constructed (in this case a book), it acts to enhance.

Craftsmanship is not an "in-group" word right now. Little

attention of a public sort is paid to a writer simply on the grounds of his mastery of materials. Of course that mastery starts with words. And I have been unable to detect on the part of our critics any great differentiation between somebody whose knowledge of words is obviously imprecise and to whom words are frozen like stones to the hand regardless of their shape, color, and so on and someone who has an obvious richness of knowledge of words—the playfulness within the word. Craftsmanship is also not particularly admired today for another reason. It is supposed to betoken an absence of creativity to a certain extent. A well-constructed piece of fiction is assumed, if it seems very neat and tight, to have lost something, to have been diminished by the writer, to have been placed on a bed of Procrustes in order to come out even with its own material, and this in itself is considered old-fashioned and probably hostile to the creative spirit.

Furthermore, our age does not care very much about craftsmanship. Most of us don't have to make very many things with our hands anymore. This is not a criticism of the way in which we live in twentieth century America, but people are conditioned by what they do with their bodies. Even though many people have returned to the land and to "natural" things, the majority of us no longer practice craftsmanship in our lives. Our food is largely prefabricated. Our clothing is almost wholly prefabricated. Our shelter is prefabricated. Our entertainment is almost all prefabricated. Most of our experience in sport is a vicarious and spectator experience. The permissive nature of our sexual morality requires very much less proficiency on our part in the whole broad spectrum of the sexual experience than in ages when things were a little tougher to get away with than they are now, and we have a crowd of helpers to raise our children. The parent-child relationship, which was I think one of the major relationships a hundred years ago, is no longer as rewarding either to the parent or the child as in good instances it was. In any event, almost everything has been removed one step away.

When it comes to craft and writing, however, you have to do it yourself. If you blow in sweet and it comes out sour, the best editor in the world cannot help you to anything more than either silence or an inoffensive mumble. So while it may not be possible to teach people much about writing, it is possible for some people to learn something about *how* to write.

This book does not offer much of a practical nature about the satisfaction of critics. At any given moment, a substantial group of the best writers of the past are always out of favor. Excellent living writers may go unremarked. Robert Frost received a notably slight amount of critical attention until his death. Every writer has, though, a large or small number of critics—the readers who read what he has written and react to it. People—a great many people— reacted to Robert Frost over a large number of years, and there is no reason to suppose they will not continue to do so.

Writing is not a road to big or easy money. Most professional writers live modestly, or they have a vogue in which they are highly paid and then fade away into a modest lifetime batting average. Nor is writing a road to fame or immortality. Fame is a many-splendored thing all right, but it is almost as rare as the phoenix. Even phoenixes have some dusty passages in their recurring life cycles.

The real rewards of writing are serious and bitter as well as sweet, like love, and they are private, not public. They range all the way from the satisfactions of good craftsmen to the inward and painful glory of a Sir Bors or a Sir Lancelot. They are not a matter of a lead review in the book section of the *New York Times*.

In some circles a ridiculous prejudice exists in favor of art at the expense of the craft out of which it develops. Academics, the bad ones, speak scornfully of "popularizing." If a thing is entertaining, in any sense, they are suspicious of its merit. The lecturer who puts his students to sleep looks with a jaundiced eye on the man who keeps them bolt upright, who tries to entertain them as he teaches so as to make what is taught memorable and colorful. The same prejudice applies in the reverse snobbery of some of the young. Writing that is not angry and impatient and "strong," writing that is at all literary or sounds as if someone else has used the same language before, is not for them.

People are not fashionable. They don't change much inside. Freud found no new complexes—to borrow a term from one of his pupils. All readers are people, and writing is always a person-to-person matter.

Probably there are other reasons for writing. As therapy. As compensation for a sense of personal inferiority. For personal pleasure—a kind of glorified crossword puzzle. And, at the other end of the scale, and very rarely, there is something indescribably and completely different. The thing that made Cezanne exclaim: "Je veux peintre des Poussins en face de la nature." But the mantle of greatness cannot be turned over to Good Will Industries for cleaning and mending and then handed along to a disadvantaged person. It is a garment that always goes into its owner's grave. He wove it and it will fit no one else.

Good writing is always positive. It is always entertaining or useful, or both. It is not a puzzle, or a sermon, or executed by a superior person for inferiors. What is written skillfully is apt to be good writing. Great writing and writers about greatness have assumed greatness in their readers. Shakespeare assumes the king and the magician and the coward and the hero in everyone. The skill and the desire to reach the reader are what carry the greatness, if it exists.

Two

BETWEEN WRITER
AND READER

Since books are my professional concern, and a lifelong one, it would be strange indeed if I did not have some pronounced opinions about literature. One of them is especially to the point here and does not seem to be discussed very much. I believe that literature is for readers, and that that is what literature is. It is not possible for critics and college professors to manufacture literature by subtlety, intricacy, special vocabulary, persuasiveness, or any of the other general tactics that they practice. The people who make a book literature are its readers, and there have to be a lot of them before a work becomes classifiable as literature. Usually about a quarter century has passed before this can happen.

And so the question of a permanent literary addition to mankind's treasurehouse is not a central concern of this book. Except in one way: if you don't get past that first verdict of your own generation, you aren't going to go any farther. It should be unnecessary to point out that there is no other court before which a writer can bring his case. There are no gods atop Mt. Olympus. The dead who have preceded us are no longer reading anything terrestrial, at least, and the future can be arrived at only through the present. Readers, almost alone, keep a writer alive after he has stopped writing. When a book is not passing under the eye of the reader, when it is on a shelf, it is nothing but ink and paper and cloth—an artifact. If it has permanence, if it is a classic, it still has no separate life. It lives only in the repeated experience of it, in the memories of those who have experienced it, and in the minds of those who come to it.

Yet I doubt if a high percentage of writers really cares about the reader. Many scarcely think of him from one chapter's end to the next, and some resent the need to do so. At one of the best-known writer's conferences, a young novelist once challenged the statement that writing was meant to be read by somebody. "I don't write for any living person," he said emphatically. "Then whom *do* you write for?" Without a second's pause the young man replied, "Posterity."

Fortunately for him, his contemporaries discovered that novelist in due course and he was widely read. In his case what posterity will do is less certain today than it was, once, in his own mind, but most of us know that the committed writer hopes to communicate with other minds across many barriers—of time, space, and language. Anyone who tries to write clearly and deeply about what he finds some part of the human experience to be like, in thought and in feeling, soon finds out that writing is hard, frustrating work; he tends to be more aware of his own strain than of his reader's future share in the process of reading. Honesty may suggest that writing is necessarily egocentric and, being so, seems to excuse a forgetfulness of the reader or of anything other than the creating self. Nevertheless, at some point, the writer must acknowledge his readers. Here, in a few words —a few lonesome and admiring and somewhat nostalgic words—I hope to introduce you to the reader and his act of reading.

I am not sure how many readers are left today in the very large society in which we live. By reader I mean another human being who is not professionally or personally involved with writers. Who is this reader I am talking about? The first thing about him is that he has learned to read. There is any God's quantity of books about this process, the problems it's making in our society, and how very, very scarred and crippled the reader may have become in the process of being taught. Let's skip over all of that, and assume he has mastered this skill to a certain extent. He is capable of looking at a printed page and finding communication in it. Let us hope he is a voluntary reader. The great mass of students who are reading fiction in this country are captive readers. It is assigned to them: Poe one day and Melville the next. This is not the kind of reader I want to talk about. The reader I am concerned with is the one who bought a magazine with your story in it, bought a book you wrote, paperback perhaps—he waited for it to come out in paperback—but in any event, he is reading whatever it is you have written, voluntarily.

The next thing about your reader that's interesting is that he doesn't care at all about you. If he's attending a class or course, he has to care at least nine sentences' worth, which can be stated later in a term paper or on an examination. But the genuine reader doesn't care whether he's reading a book written by a man or a woman, by somebody young or old, or if it was written yesterday or two hundred years ago. Furthermore, he isn't there to be improved by you. He isn't saying, "Tell me, dear author, about yourself and what you think about the world, art, life, the eternal verities." What he is saying is so frightening that I urge you not to think about it while you are writing—you may get a kind of palsy. What he is saying is, "Tell me about me. I want to be more alive. Give me *me*." All the great fiction of the world satisfies this need: it tells me about me. That's what's good about Shakespeare and it's also what's good about Homer. Shakespeare—except when you get hold of a book called "The Doctored Works of Shakespeare" or something of the sort—tells you absolutely nothing about himself. You can't learn anything about Shakespeare in Shakespeare. He, himself, is in dispute among scholars and critics to this very day because all he ever wrote about was you and me. Tell me about me.

Montaigne, in his essay, "Of Bookes," speaking of himself as a reader, said, in the Florio translation:

> If in reading I fortune to meet with any difficult points, I fret not my selfe upon them, but after I have given them a charge or two, I leave them as I found them. Should I

earnestly plod upon them, I should lose both time and my selfe; for I have a skipping wit. What I see not at the first view, I shall lesse see it, if I opinionate my selfe upon it. . . . If one booke seeme tedious to me, I take another, which I follow not with any earnestness, except it be at such houres as I am idle, or that I am weary with doing nothing.

For such a reader, the identification of symbols, the identification of themes, the identification of significances is unimportant; he is a selfish reader in a very pure sense. A true act of reading is quite possibly the reverse of scanning words professionally, as practiced by the critic. The critic is analyzing and diagnosing and studying, and he is all the while carrying on a complicated process, which, at the risk of oversimplification, I shall describe as reading for the writer and writing for the reader. The real reader is not studying anything, he is not noticing anything. He is simply rapt. He is absorbed. He is unaware of the writer or of his other self.

Watch a child's body when he is reading if you want to see the real reader. He wants to get on with the "story," to be caught up in it, to become it, to take it into himself. In the process he may find much more, but he does so through that delight that is the highest form of entertainment.

For me "that delight" means a kind of inner celebration, joyful in a deep sense; an act of receiving from outside a gift, which, by the nature of its reception, makes me more human and less personal. It means also participating in the experience that the work of art is. There is in it an element of evocation, something good coming out of myself, and an element of growth, of becoming. The whole experience is pleasurable, and perhaps it contains an element of religion.   .

The responses worth having come from readers who are participating almost to the point of loss of personal identity. Too little is known, however, of what the reader does to the words he is reading—the extent to which he augments or collaborates—to describe with any assurance how this participation is brought about. Clearly the process depends upon memory—the reader is being reminded—and upon recognition, which is perhaps a memory function. But for arbitrary symbols on paper to be able to pluck at the stored riches in each reader requires an intricate act of translation. I once commissioned an article on this subject from a research psychologist and got a fascinating essay on neural objects. Technical jargon. But if you will look at a piece of paper in front of you and pretend you are writing on it while somebody else is looking over your shoulder reading what you write, perhaps we can see what is going on.

To begin with, nobody knows where what you decide to write comes from, or in what shape it first emerges; whether it is a dreamlike image or a constellation of nonverbal, sensory material. But in the course of this creative process something emerges, and your mind translates this into words. It does exactly what a translator does when he is wrestling with a difficult text. It runs over a number of possibilities and makes its selection, word for word, from the entire available vocabulary in its storehouse. In short, it translates the original material, whatever it was, into a sequence of words.

Now the reverse process is going on in the mind of the

person who is reading those words. The symbols come in through the eye, go back through the optic nerve, and after they have passed through the reader's conscious mind, they go into some repository in his memory where, for all we know, they are stored in a form not at all like words. It may be a form similar to that which first emerged in the writer's mind.

The process is so complicated and so dependent upon the reading half of the equation that it is obvious that the writer must rely upon the nearly total similarity of the reader to himself, just as the reader must rely upon the notion that he can understand the writer as a human almost identical to *himself*. The reader must have the same kinds of connections in his mind and in his memory, in his whole sensing apparatus, in order to rebuild something like what the writer wrote. It is contrary to everything we know about the structure of the universe to suppose that any artist or writer can implant in the inward sensibility of another human being anything that isn't already there—even embryonically. He rearranges it, stimulates it, causes it to go through new channels.

Fiction is necessarily based on elements that the writer and the reader have in common—language, sexuality—basic experiences both physiological and psychological. Consider also: sense of humor, sense of the group, sense of triumph and defeat, awareness of pain and death, many direct physical memories—hunger, thirst, exhaustion. The writer of fiction seeks to create within his reader a climate in which he can grow these reactions.

Perhaps the easiest way of putting it is to say that the

writer involves his reader by creating an illusion of reality. Admittedly, this reality must be very different from life itself—limited, narrow, sensorily incomplete. But a part can stand for the whole. A pocket knife can "tell" the story of a whole culture. The stronger this illusion of reality, the more completely it engrosses the entire conscious attention of the reader.

I do not know if this illusion is merely a reader's illusion. I doubt if it is. The writer probably shares in it. Is going to a concert an illusion? If so, of what? Is looking at a painting an illusion? If so, what is it an illusion of? Of oneself? Of God? These are impossible questions to answer. I believe that fiction is as much of a reality as any other experience that the reader undertakes. Call it vicarious if you like, but the reader is not a spectator, he is a participant. A novel can make you laugh or cry or go looking for someone you crave. These things are so real they are physiological. Vicarious? Perhaps, but not disembodied.

Thus, between writer and reader there is a communication, but how intricate, how complex, how inexplicable. That which is creative in the writer is necessarily matched by a creativity in the reader. In expository writing the level may be no more profound than mere intellectual response. But in drama and poetry and fiction it is very deep, perhaps subliminal.

The matter does not rest there, however, because—and even more basic—each new reader is, for the writer, a new coauthor. To the child-reader the story has no author. The story exists in itself and the child consumes it like ice cream or cake, fiercely, personally. But each and every mature reader brings his own special conditioning to everything he reads. So do the generations. Witness the changes in critical approach from century to century and even from decade to decade. Not only that, the same reader, at different ages, brings different responses to the same book. In his *Writer's Notebook,* Somerset Maugham says it this way: "It is sad, indeed, to reread something which at one time had made one to feel like Keats's Watcher in the Skies and be forced to the admission that after all it's not much."

The greatest works, then, are those that can survive the years and a change from one language into another. We are all aware of how much is lost to time and translation: many jokes, most contemporary allusions, various religious and artistic dimensions, and even word meanings.

So, "writing" in the sense in which it is used here means something considerably more than the mere setting down of words on paper. It means eliciting responses. It means accepting the reader as a more than passive coauthor of the work as it comes into its true life.

Now back to our real, unprofessional reader in his freedom not to read, and what it is the writer wants from him. First, of course, continuation. Staying with the work of writing to the end. A complete experience of it. The turning of page after page. Second, assent. At the least a reading that is not hostile, scornful, condescending, inappropriate in any way. Third, intensity. The writer wants the reader to pay attention to him and him only. Fourth, understanding. At worst this can mean wanting to improve the reader. At best, it means a sharing so full that at the end, the experience belongs both to the writer who wrote it in his mind and then outwardly to the reader, and to the reader who received it through fearfully abstract symbols and reproduced it in his own imagination. It is this collaboration that completes the experience.

Three

FICTION AND THE
MEANS OF PERCEPTION

The disciplines of fiction are few in number, but they are all basic, and not one of them is thoroughly accepted or understood by unsuccessful writers of fiction. Among these unsuccessful writers are many who are published. Publication is not necessarily a sign of success.

The best book review page on the West Coast once published a feature article. Here are the first three paragraphs of that article:

> Granted, you can't tell a book by its cover. But you can tell a book worth reading by its title and the first sentences.
>
> Gushing onto the market this winter and spring—like an artesian well of printed words—are a mob of new literate voices babbling to be heard behind the brilliantly illustrated covers of hundreds of books.

> For the most part, these new novels . . . are destined for bargain table piles unsold at 50 cents a copy. Even at that reduced price they are no bargain. The authors, while quite able to put one English word after another, have, in total, nothing to say, and the people they write about are as worthless and uninteresting as gum wrappers in the gutter.

The author of this blast goes on to cite a number of novels and their opening sentences, comparing them with the first sentences of books by the masters of fiction, Faulkner, Hemingway, and Algren, to name three. Not one of the openings cited as atrocious was by a writer who has subsequently achieved his or her own readership.

Those first sentences of a novel are a contract between the writer of fiction and the reader who commences to read him. The contract has to be clear almost at once. What does the writer contract to do in those crucial sentences? Several things that are, taken together, the core of the fictional process. First, he contracts to tell a story, not necessarily a highly plotted one, but a story. Second, he promises that the story will be told in terms of people, and most usually in terms of scenes, not descriptions. Third, he promises that there will be an end, just as there is, in front of the reader's eyes, a beginning. And that adds up to a promise of some kind of fictional action—narration, conflict, change, and resolution.

What does the reader contract to do? Simply to read, and in so doing to share the experience. This contract constantly has to be renewed as a work of fiction progresses. And this is accomplished mainly by the author's use of technical devices upon which the reader subconsciously relies.

One of the principal techniques is the use of a character whom the reader adopts for his reading experience. In the best fiction and most of the time, the reader is identifying with one or another of the characters in the story. He is vicariously living the fictional life of that character. He is *being* the Ishmael of *Moby Dick*. He is *being* the narrator of *Deliverance*. He is not, be it noted, being either Herman Melville or James Dickey.

This is a difficult notion for some writers. No adequate terms exists for this character the reader becomes. In his book *The World of Fiction,* Bernard DeVoto called this character "the means of perception." It makes little difference what he is called; whether one uses the term "point of view," "standpoint," "alter ego," or "reader identification," is not important. What is important is that this is the fiction writer's most useful device for securing his reader's participation. Experiencing a work of fiction through one of its characters is the all-absorbing, self-obliterating joy of reading. It is the core of the child's experience. Who has never been Alice in Wonderland, or Winnie the Pooh, or Jim Hawkins in the apple barrel on his way to Treasure Island?

The easiest way to understand how this technique works is to consider a novel or a story written in the first person singular. Everything in the story is perceived by a single narrator. The story can contain nothing that the narrator does not know. Other characters tell him things and, as in the case of Maugham's *The Moon and Sixpence,* much of the action may take place far from the narrator, but it all has to be told to the reader through a single source. Chapter One begins:

> I confess that when first I made acquaintance with Charles Strickland I never for a moment discerned that there was in him anything out of the ordinary.

Report, dialogue, inference, deduction, many kinds of clues are useful, but the reader is from beginning to end experiencing the book through a single mind.

A second approach to the means of perception is through the third person singular. Here the reader identifies himself with one character, or with one character at a time, and experiences the story through that character. This is perhaps the commonest of fictional forms. Hemingway's *The Old Man and the Sea* begins:

> He was an old man who fished alone in a skiff in the Gulf Stream and he had gone eighty-four days now without taking a fish.

Notice that the means of perception is instantly established and that the reader is already halfway over the gunwale and into that small skiff out in the Gulf Stream.

With rare and tricky exceptions, there is in successful fiction one and only one means of perception to a scene. This singleness is tremendously important in dialogue, especially when a number of characters are on stage. It is a temptation for the writer to hop into one mind after another as his characters talk. To write successful dialogue the author must have access to the mind of all his characters, but the reader must not perceive any more than he would in real life. We all hear conversations with our own ears only. By the same token, all the scenes of our individual lives are perceived by us singly and separately. All of us are persons who have never been anybody but ourselves, and if a writer can tell his story in terms of only one vicarious self the reader can become submerged deeper in the story than if he has to surface to change age, condition, and even sex. Life deals out to each of us one, and only one, means of perception.

The glory of fiction is that it gives us the effect of being someone else. This is the human reason why the means of perception is central to the experience of reading fiction.

So, the fiction writer is faced with the problem of deciding who, from the reader's point of view, is telling the story: a narrator—the "I" story—in which case the reader, following the story, simply becomes the fictional character who is the narrator; a central character who is told about by the writer, but as if the writer were serving for the reader; a series of characters, each of whom, in turn, perceives for the reader; or a nevernamed and omniscient narrator. (Many an author would wish this last to be the case all the time. Oddly enough, however, in terms of narrative approach, the omniscient narrator is a position impossible to sustain.) There are other choices, but the question one must always ask is, who is the reader *being* as he reads?

The selection of the narrative approach or means of perception is one of the first things a fiction writer must do if he wants to be read. His selection should be a conscious or accurate one, and it must be made scene by scene, chapter by chapter, or book by book. Thereafter, he must shape his entire narration in terms of that decision. This point cannot be ignored. To ignore it is to forget the reader. The reader must always understand on any page in any sentence at any word—at any single word—the nature of his relationship to the story.

Many writers vigorously resist this concept of the means of perception and with it the notion of reader identification. They point to the nineteenth century novelists—to Dickens and Thackeray and Scott for whom the book habitually served as a kind of rostrum—and to other great exceptions. One can admit that it is tempting to play God with the reader, to describe everything—the narrative itself, the characters, the settings, even the meaning. But only a great writer should take a chance on getting away with this, and only the really great writers succeed. Trollope interrupts his tale of the fortunes of *Ralph the Heir* to acknowledge this:

> It is the test of a novel writer's art that he conceals his snake-in-the-grass; but the reader may be sure that it is always there. No man or woman with a conscience, no man or woman with intellect sufficient to produce amusement, can go on from year to year spinning stories without the desire of teaching; with no ambition of influencing readers for their own good. Gentle readers, the physic is always beneath the sugar, hidden or unhidden. In writing novels we novelists preach to you from our pulpits, and are keenly anxious that our sermons shall not be inefficacious. Inefficacious they are not, unless they be too badly preached to

obtain attention. Injurious they will be unless the lessons taught be good lessons.

Anything a writer does that deepens reader involvement strengthens the fiction. Everything, especially the author's voice, that corrupts this identification damages the illusion of fiction. The reader may not immediately be aware of the damage, but like the hours on the old sundial motto: "Omnia vulnerant, ultima necat."

This is a hard gospel to live by. What is the alternative? The captive reader? A convention that must be adhered to, like a minuet? A celebration in which each writer is a part of God Himself, choired by the cherubim and seraphim who read him?

Take an example from a manuscript submitted but not likely to see publication:

He did not feel very professorial. But that did not worry him. What rather invited his criticism lay in the haunting question: "How, actually, do I stack up as a teacher?" In reality, it did not bother him so much in the classroom. Once in action, there was no self-consciousness left. It was only as he circulated in the open like this—vulnerable to the naked energy of giant-sized collective youth—that he conceived a certain dread. His own appearance was worn but youthful as he strode along the street, his briefcase swinging like a pendant beside him, a pendant as distinctive of his breed as the battered lunchpail swinging beside the man with a shovel and pickaxe.

What is going on here? The author is talking *at* us. He is, in effect, lecturing. The reader is constantly aware of the author. Take a look at the actual words. The beginning is all right. We know immediately that our means of perception is a professor, and almost immediately that he is worried. But then we read: "What rather invited his criticism. . . ." Is our character saying to himself, "What rather invites my criticism. . . ."? No. The author is beginning to intrude himself. And whose phrase is "In reality, . . ."? The author's. Simply "It did not bother him so much. . . ." would be better. Go on to "—vulnerable to the naked energy of giant-sized collective youth—" Again the author talking, and in a vocabulary appropriate to a course in sociology. Thereafter, he abandons any attempt to write from within his character and describes in his own words what he wants us to see. Finally, adding insult to injury already done his fiction, he cannot resist the temptation to give us his own analogy: "as distinctive of his breed as. . . ." We are far afield now and the author makes it exceedingly difficult for us to get back from "the man with a shovel and pickaxe" to the mind of his troubled professor.

It is a constructive exercise for the fiction writer to read over his or her own fiction manuscript, cutting out every paragraph, every sentence, every word where the author has briefed the reader—told him rather than shown him something the author wants him to know so that he can get on with the story—and then to survey what is left and discover when the reader finds out which character is to be the means of perception in each new scene. The sooner the better—the grace period is short. We have all experienced the annoyance of the telephone call from an unfamiliar voice that does not identify itself.

Fiction and the Means of Perception

More fiction fails because the author has not had the discipline and the ingenuity to provide and sustain a means of perception than for any other single reason. That is an editorial opinion, not a statistic.

Editor's note: The following excerpts from letters show how W.S. tried to get this point across.

To Ernest K. Gann, October 17, 1947, "Notes on *Benjamin Lawless*":

First, you know that every novel is an illusion of reality which the reader accepts as real as long as he is immersed in the book. Your reader has got to live in this illusion which you are creating for him in this opening chapter. You are a story-teller to him, and you have got to stick by the implied contract, which is that you are telling him a story which he accepts as real.

Now it follows that the reader has got to "get" the story through some channel or other. Some people call this point of view and others "means of perception." But I think you can write it down as a hard-and-fast rule that in all novels written today this *means of perception* is never never never the author himself. You cannot talk *at* the reader the way the nineteenth century boys could. You cannot ever *tell* the reader anything, you have got to *show* him, and through the means of perception that you are employing. (In this book, the principal means of perception are your four chief characters, and while others have perhaps been used, the closer we stick to these four the better the book will be. Four is enough, and there should be no others except for occasional dramatic emphasis.) I can't put it too strongly that the reader's sense of reality from the book hangs on this rule.

To Albert E. Idell (the letter is undated, but his novel, *Stephen Hayne,* was subsequently published in 1951):

Let me admit right here that there are exceptions to every rule. A kind of light social comedy or mild satire can survive a good many violations of these rules about the means of perception. If the violations are in the same tone of voice as the actual story, and if their purpose is the same. Thus, you can describe a Victorian parlor before anyone comes into it. That would be you talking at the reader, but it is, well done, still a case of showing not telling, and books of that sort are in a sense written to be read at arm's length. But serious fiction, involving the reader's whole attention and sympathies, cannot survive too many ruptures of the fabric of illusion by which this attention and sympathy are captured.

In your own writing, particularly with this novel, you do a great many small things, and a few larger ones, to violate an illusion which you have been at skill and pains to create. Take the second scene in the book—the tavern scene. Your means of perception here is Stephen. The reader is intended to perceive it all through his eyes and ears. As he enters the room, you are all right: ". . . Stephen glanced around the low-ceilinged room. Among the men sitting on the bent hickory chairs were several who knew him. [This is all right only if you mean that Stephen thought of people in that way—as knowing him or not knowing him, rather than the more usual pattern of men whom he knew or did not

Fiction and the Means of Perception

know, as most people do. If you don't mean the sentence as characterizing Stephen, then it is you, the author, telling me that some of the men knew your character, when you could just as easily have Stephen—at this moment I *am* Stephen—recognize them.] Unconsciously, he swaggered a trifle, filling out his chest and causing his elbows to jut out, etc." Now you've torn it. Can you see what that word "unconsciously" has done to me as the reader? The small ambiguity of the point of view in the sentence before is suddenly multipled a dozen times. Now I cannot be Stephen again until you recreate the illusion. Now I am a spectator at the book and not a participant of it. You are not showing me; you are telling me.

Thereupon you go on in a manner that makes it hard for me to rejoin the story safely. "The occupants of the bar gazed at him curiously, etc." Who thought they were gazing curiously? Stephen? Then make it so. If not, it is the author again.

Four

FICTION AND
THE NARRATIVE PROCESS

So far as we have recorded evidence, storytelling—or narration—is the oldest kind of literature. It was old when Homer first told the story of the anger of Achilles and the result of that anger. Storytelling is the way a child learns the delight of the language, of the world of words, and of the bridge words build between people. Storytelling is also the way the gods have spoken, with the parables of the New Testament as a supreme example. Narration is, indeed, an overwhelmingly large part of the daily dialogues we have with each other, and we exchange narrative anecdotes as a kind of game. This narrative organization that we give to almost every sort of experience is expressed in countless ways: "So-and-so's life story" or "that's the story of my life." Or, "a tale told by an idiot/Full of sound and fury, signifying nothing. . . ."

For a while, not so long ago, this storytelling characteristic that pervades human life was relegated by critics to a minor position, running far behind such matters as symbolism, social significance, and various forms of philosophy and self-philosophizing. Fiction is not philosophy or poetry or intimations either of mortality or immortality. It is not sociology, or the revelation of truth. Often it is concerned with these things, but this comes across primarily by entertaining. Consider the plays of G. B. Shaw in comparison with the works of Hegel. Entertainment is a quality we do not treasure enough in our contemporary reading and writing. Significance is a dry crust without it, protest is both ugly and violent without it. Neither can be widely communicated without it.

As an editor I believe I have learned this much about the narrative faculty in a writer: it cannot be taught. Its techniques can be discussed—foreshadowing, for instance, or the structure of scenes in fiction and nonfiction, perhaps even "plotting"—but there is a special quality about a writer with the narrative gift. He makes you want to read on, to find out what is going to happen. Teaching cannot create this quality nor conceal its absence, but perhaps where it exists it can be strengthened and understood.

I am also convinced that successful fiction is impossible without storytelling of some kind. Perhaps the farthest it could hope to go is a fascinating and arrogantly superficial piece of writing like Hemingway's "The Sea Change." This self-conscious slice of life becomes tolerable because of the artistry of its construction and, even more important, because the reader has already read so much Hemingway that the vignette fits into the Hemingway continuum, and is propped up at each end, and shored in the middle, too, by the rest of Hemingway the reader has read. "The Sea Change" *is* a poignant piece of writing. The only thing that isn't there is the story. Hemingway could fall back on his reputation, but for beginning writers it's best to have a story.

Narrative is not an easy thing to define. One way of getting at it is to say that it is all that part of a manuscript that answers three basic questions. What has happened? What is happening? What is going to happen? Viewed in this rather general light a novel no longer has to have what used to be called plot. It does have to have two things that serve the same function. It has to have narrative and structure. These two elements should not exist as separate and disparate ingredients. They are utterly fused from beginning to end.

We have all been bored to distraction by people who tell stories badly. One thing we sometimes say is "begin at the beginning, for Pete's sake." This tells us a lot about how the auditor or reader receives a story. He wants a structure, and the first part of the structure that he wants is a beginning. Any beginning implies an end. The reader does not care how much the author may juggle the time within the novel. The author can flash backwards in time or leap forward, he can move sideways—"meanwhile, back at the ranch"—or he can circle a single fleeting instant, but however he goes about it, he goes about it within a structure.

Between beginning and end, everything in the novel happens, everything must happen. What happens could be called the process of the novel. By way of contrast, a dictionary also has a process, but it is wholly an alphabetical process, from aardvark to zoril. When a dictionary runs out of letters it stops. There is something of an analogy here, because when a novel completes its process it, too, stops. There should be nothing left over, and the old-fashioned epilogue telling what happened to the character in later life should be the exception rather than the rule.

The process of the novel is usually discussed in terms of narrative motion, action, plot, cumulative structure, and so on. By "process" I mean progression and action.

The core of the process is change. Things are not the same at the end of the novel as they were at the beginning. What is it that changes? The answer is, almost everything. Characters change, relationships change, conflicts change. In a subtle way the meaning of words central to the novel changes. The title *The Grapes of Wrath* is, at first, a quotation from "The Battle Hymn of the Republic," but by the novel's end it has overtones of life, a way of life, and death. Settings change, even time scales change. A large part of the process of the novel resides in these changes. Consider their many variations in *The Turn of the Screw, Jane Eyre,* Conrad's *Lord Jim,* and Wallace Stegner's *Angle of Repose.*

When does the process commence? When the direction of its course becomes certain to the writer and at least unconsciously so to the reader. If there is to be a prologue section, the process must be working in it. A good beginning establishes not only time, setting, means of perception, tone of voice, and scale—scale does not mean length so much as depth—but it also establishes the fact that something is going to happen. James M. Cain's *The Postman Always Rings Twice* commences, "They threw me off the hay cart about noon." All the ingredients are in lively evidence and off and running. A good beginning, however, is not enough. After the process has started, it cannot be halted or interrupted. This means that the change, though its rate may be controlled, must be a continuous reaction. Like a fire, it can smolder or blaze, but it cannot go out. A piece of fiction begins when the writer scratches the match, not when he lays the fire. It ends when all the logs have become ashes.

So process is both motion and consumption, and the factors that lead a reader forward are his sense of process, of motion, the recognition of change brought about by that motion, an unrealized feeling of inevitability: "Thus it was and had to be." Obviously, the primary mode of this motion, the primary aspect of this process is the interaction of the people—the characters—in the work of fiction. Interaction in action, in dialogue, in circumstance. These human interactions are the only matter of fiction.

What the novelist has to say has to be said through his characters. He is not going to be forgiven by his reader for stopping his story to lecture. The reader doesn't care what the man or woman whose name is on the title page thinks about the arms race or premarital chastity or life on Mars or automation. He does care what the characters think about these things if they act upon their thoughts and interact upon the other characters because of them.

Other elements spur the reader along: for example, a sense of danger. This can be induced by the technique of foreshadowing, overt or concealed. It takes skill, however, and is not to be done by the "had-I-but-known" type of machinery. It may be effected by the introduction of an unstable character, or by the use of action details that the reader will see must lead on to something else. The classic illustration here is the device of the letter in *Tess of the D'Urbervilles*. But foreshadowing is best accomplished by some way in which the characters themselves are legitimately aware that something is about to happen. Early in Henry James' novel *Roderick Hudson,* the reader is warned of tragedy by the character's own sense of foreboding:

> He sat up beside his companion and looked away at the far-spreading view, which affected him as melting for them both into such vast continuities and possibilities of possession. It touched him to the heart; suddenly a strange feeling of prospective regret took possession of him. Something seemed to tell him that later, in a foreign land, he should be haunted by it, should remember it all with longing and regret.

And in James Dickey's *Deliverance,* the narrator foreshadows the nightmare consequences of the river by these lines:

> A slow force took hold of us; the bank began to go backward. I felt the complicated urgency of the current, like a thing of many threads being pulled, and with this came the feeling I always had at the moment of losing consciousness at night, going toward something unknown that I could not avoid, but from which I would return.

Fiction and the Narrative Process

Movement toward a known event can be heightened by the device of a frame. A novel may start with the actual circumstances of its own end, like the death of a character.

Editor's note: In a letter of January 24, 1960, W.S. wrote to Richard Wormser, who was at work on his novel, *Battalion of Saints:*

> All frames serve a purpose, and part of the purpose is to serve as a kind of foreshadowing. They demonstrate to the reader that in the book he is entering something happens, that there has been action, and conflict between people, and that something has moved in time between one point and another. They introduce the reader to some of the characters. They generate anticipation—a curiosity as to what led up to all this.

Finally, forward motion in any piece of writing is carried by verbs. Verbs are the action words of the language and the most important. Turn to any passage on any page of a successful novel and notice the high percentage of verbs. Beginning writers always use too many adjectives and adverbs and generally use too many dependent clauses. Count your words and words of verbal force (like that word "force" I just used).

Avoid like the plague the use of clichés. They are motion killers. Here are a few samples from a schoolteacher novel I have been reading: "a premonition of autumn in the air," "waited with anticipation," "but for a few faded bulletins," "in keeping with the general excitement," "vibrant with her joy of being alive," "bespoke dignity and poise," "secretly amused," "look in vain," "echoed through the empty corridors," "rapidly becoming a nightmare," "dire consequences." Clichés are miserable because they summon up nothing.

Know what each and every word you use means. Look them up in the dictionaries, especially the ones with good etymologies. There is no substitute for knowing words. Love words. Love language. Read about the English language. Read all about it. Get hold of the Strunk and White essay on style and you better believe it. Own and read Fowler.

Exercise your words. Try them out in new relationships. When you write anything—road directions or recipes or letters, try seeing if you can manage to bring a grin to the face of the person reading your workaday words. Study wit. Wit is basically a play with words.

Stay away from everything that is fancy or pretty or grandiloquent: "Illumination is required to be extinguished in this premises at the conclusion of business." This means: "Storelights must be put out at the end of the day."

Eschew—the word comes to us from Middle English and from the French *eschiver* which in turn comes from the Latin *vite vitare,* to avoid or shun, and one of its cousins once-removed is the word "shy"—eschew verbal tricks of all kinds. Every awkwardness that brings the reader up short gives him two unpleasant reminders, however subliminally —the reminder of study and the reminder that he is reading words instead of living vicariously.

Editor's note: The following excerpt is from "Notes on Chapter Four" to Ernest K. Gann, whose novel *Benjamin Lawless,* W.S. was editing:

Fiction and the Narrative Process

This is a tough chapter. There's nothing big wrong with it, but there are a whole lot of little things that sap the total effect. You have point of view trouble. The writing is often amateurish, and you use pretentious phrases and large generalizing words instead of the smaller, sharp, homespun words that would be natural to Ben. . . . Avoid words like "almost," try to avoid the passive voice in your verbs . . . "His blue eyes commanded their interest . . . seemed fixed upon some distant object . . . pursuing someone . . . many felt obliged . . . experienced a sense of disappointment" is all bad writing, sawdust stuff. Damn it, Gann, when you get off the beam you get rhetorical as hell, and just full of clichés . . . "For what seemed an eternity"—! No!

Afterthoughts, explanatory flashbacks, author's essays, description for the sake of itself rather than for the fiction, dialogue that leads nowhere, characters who do not contribute to the action, violation of the means of perception, confusion of the reader by any means—a thousand such crudities are the enemies of the fictional process.

Another enemy is the conscious striving for "style." No word is dearer to some critics and some writers than the word "style." Millions of students who haven't the slightest idea what their instructors mean by the word are exposed to it. Lecturers use the word with a casualness that is awe-inspiring: "The style of the early Hemingway" or "In a sense the style of the later Henry James may be said to . . ."

This leads writers into the frustrating idea that a style is something you acquire. Well, that's true of tennis and piano playing and seduction—all ways in which a particular person does a particular thing. But the glorious thing about the writing game is that if you learn to play it you will develop style. And who cares if you do not? Styles are neither good nor bad, intrinsically. For a writer, the only question is how his developing style grows out of his writing, not how it is implanted in it. A style that recreates the writer's own tone of voice for the reader is the ultimate result of the best writing. Nathaniel Hawthorne, in 1851, wrote to an editor:

> I am glad you think my style plain. I never, in any one page or paragraph, aimed at making it anything else, or giving it any other merit—and I wish people would leave off talking about its beauty. If it have any, it is only pardonable as being unintentional. The greatest possible merit of style is, of course, to make the words absolutely disappear into the thought.

The best way to start on style is the hard way, the way Gertrude Stein was, I believe, trying to explain to Hemingway. Start clean and simple. Don't try to write pretty or noble or big or anything like that. Try to say just what you mean. This is hard because you have to find out what you mean, and that's work, real work.

Editor's note: From an editorial letter to Ernest K. Gann— "Notes on *Benjamin Lawless,* Chapter Six":

> In trying to tell you what is wrong with the writing here I come up against a nearly indescribable thing. You have your own style. You don't write like everybody else. When you are on your own beam, your stuff is fresh and alive. It has a vitality and charm which is something like that of a

Fiction and the Narrative Process

child after he or she has learned to talk and before he or she has learned to talk just like everybody else. I don't want you to lose that quality, which is a part of the armament of a good storyteller.

But all too often this quality curdles on you. It wanders off into big words imprecisely used, into "literary" words, into sonority or affectation or inflation or gaucheries of one kind or another. Except for the top half of page 75, this whole treatment of Betty is spoiled by these faults: "multitude of scents" "savored for a price" "normal confinement" "discovered their way" "delicate distractions", and so on. These add up to a mannered and self-conscious piece of prose, but they aren't Gann, they aren't Betty and they are not *Benjamin Lawless,* a novel.

Read this stuff aloud to yourself in some private spot and you will see what I mean. It is Gann being playful with the reader. There is more than one way to break the means of perception. One way is to be so self-conscious and mannered about the style that you inevitably remind the reader that this is a piece of writing. If you can avoid this you are far more likely "to affect the life of another quite as much as your own."

Look, I am not trying to get you to write with the cold precision of an encyclopedist or the flavorless facility of a low-grade hack. I am not trying to excise the humor which underlies some of this overblown writing of yours, when it occurs. I just object to putting shots of cherry coke into good wine.

Finally, one must say a few words about the novel of plot versus the novel of theme. It should be a term of approbation to speak of a "well-plotted" novel. Some people regard plot as an artificiality, as hampering and shackling to full expression, as a technical device that has been exhausted—"there are no new plots"—and otherwise consider plot unnecessary.

Nevertheless the novel of plot has some durable and perhaps inexhaustible advantages. In its simpler forms—the western, the mystery story, a lot of science fiction—it has never lost its power to entertain. A plotted novel moves forward, it has narrative motion. The very development of its plot entertains the reader both by surprising him and presenting him with the inevitable. There is often a chase of some sort or other in a highly plotted novel, and there is likely to be a good deal of action.

The novel of theme, on the other hand, tends to rely upon a psychological structure. "The theme of *Lord of the Flies*," says William Golding, its author, "is an attempt to trace the defects of society back to the defects of human nature." We may accept that if we like, but the sentence does not explain why *Lord of the Flies* is a novel at all, and the statement would apply equally well to Menninger's *Man Against Himself,* which is no novel. In a novel of theme, the characters are apt to assume symbolic overtones and the scenes or events to be put together for the sake of the theme.

But even with the novel of theme, there is no possible charter of emancipation from all rules of technique. The novel of theme commences when the novelist is ready to start on the theme. *Lord of the Flies* does not begin with a description of society. Not even with the flight of the airplane, which crashes and spews those symbolic children all over that conveniently designed island. A novel, in short, begins at the point where the novelist commences *showing*

Fiction and the Narrative Process

the reader, not explaining something to him. A human life starts at birth, though elements of it may and do precede that moment. In any novel, the end is implicit in the beginning, and the beginning validates the end.

No matter which approach (plot or theme) the novelist elects, he must answer the reader's question of "what happens?" The reader is not reading to expose himself to the novelist and admire the writer; he is reading on his own behalf and from an interest in his own inner and outer worlds.

When does the novel end? It ends when it has consumed its own material, the actions terminated, the tensions resolved. Just as there must be nothing truly superfluous in a novel, so there must be nothing left over after it ends. The reader will always know that terrible moment when the lights have dimmed down and the curtain fallen. It is no use standing in front of the curtain and talking at him.

Five

SCENE

The keystone of all fiction is the scene. The fictional scene
is the mode or way in which the writer speaks to the reader.
The fictional scene is the way in which the story happens. It
is also the way in which the reader experiences the novel or
story. In its pure essence, a work of fiction is a sequence of
scenes from page one to the end. But life does not come
to us packaged in a series of scenes. It is up to the writer to
package it. In a brilliant passage in his later introduction
to his first novel, *Roderick Hudson,* Henry James tries to
explain how the writer translates the material of life into the
convention of scene.

> Really, universally, relations stop nowhere, and the ex-
> quisite problem of the artist is eternally but to draw, by a
> geometry of his own, the circle within which they shall hap-

pily *appear* to do so. He is in the perpetual predicament that the continuity of things is the whole matter, for him, of comedy and tragedy; that this continuity is never, by the space of an instant or an inch, broken, and that, to do anything at all, he has at once intensely to consult and intensely to ignore it.

James goes on to describe, by a metaphor, the way in which he worked at this problem:

. . . a young embroiderer of the canvas of life soon began to work in terror, fairly, of the vast expanse of that surface, of the boundless number of distinct perforations for the needle, and of the tendency inherent in his many-coloured flowers and figures to cover and consume as many as possible of the little holes. The development of the flower, of the figure, involved thus an immense counting of holes and a careful selection among them. That would have been, it seemed to him, a brave enough process, were it not the very nature of the holes so to invite, solicit, to persuade, to practise positively a thousand lures and deceits. The prime effect of so sustained a system, so prepared a surface, is to lead on and on; while the fascination of following resides, by the same token in the presumability *somewhere* of a convenient, or a visibly-appointed stopping-place.

What is a scene? A scene is a unit of event which has a beginning, a middle, and an end, and it contains nothing except characters in action. In the theater, which resembles fiction in that the entire substance of a play is what goes on between people, a scene begins each time the curtain rises or a character comes on stage or goes off stage. A scene ends when the curtain falls or when the onstage cast is diminished or augmented.

This is almost directly applicable to fiction. But in fiction it is vital to know what a scene is *not*. It is not the author telling the reader something, like, say, how the sunset looked. Looked to whom? In short, scene is not briefing. Scene is not a tone poem intended to evoke a mood or to simulate poetry in prose. Scene is not material written for its own sake—a clever aside for the fun of it, a comment on the way life is. Scene is not material written prior to the necessary start of the action or following after the interaction of the characters has been completed. If a piece of fiction contains passages with such characteristics, these passages are unfictional at least and probably nonfictional.

Many unsuccessful writers have difficulty believing the simple point of *showing, not telling.* They believe in a sort of Divine Right of Kings by which the fiction writer can choose whether he is going to show or to tell. No such right exists. Once I was sitting on my terrace with Shane Stevens, novelist, critic, Bread Loaf Fellow. He was explaining to me that my cat, which he was stroking, was actually a duck in a catsuit zippered over her.

"You're not listening," he accused me.

I explained that I was trying to think out my next fiction lecture, and the next.

"Where are you going to begin?" he enquired.

I told him with scene, and that I thought everything in

fiction had to be conveyed to the reader by way of scenes.

He scratched the duck-cat behind her ears. "You better believe it," he said.

What Shane and I had created was a scene that *shows* what we both meant better than any amount of explanation possibly could. More seriously, let me remind you of what we all subconsciously know. The scenes of fiction are what readers remember when they are not remembering the characters. "I'll never forget that scene in *David Copperfield*." they say. Or, "That was a great scene where Tom got the other fellow to whitewash the fence." Admittedly, it is trouble for the writer to find the scenes he needs and to load them with the ammunition of his fiction, but it can be done. There is nothing that belongs in fiction at all that cannot be conveyed to the reader by way of a real and lively scene.

The number of possible scenes is infinite, of course, but the writer needs to know two things in order to *select* the ones best suited to his purpose. These two things have to be *found out,* and they are so often mishandled by unsuccessful writers that every editor gets a kind of second sight about them. The instant he is sure the writer has failed to meet these two requirements, he will reject the manuscript.

First, the author has to know what his book is about. Maybe the reader doesn't need to realize this overtly, but he has to feel he is finding out. If the author doesn't know, or knows mistakenly—which is very often the case—the book or story will fail. All too many stories and novels are inert. Mostly, this inertness occurs because the author doesn't know what his story is—or is simply infatuated with the sound of his own writing voice.

Scene

The writer must know also *what happens* in his book. If he does he is past the second hurdle. No piece of fiction can survive the dullness of nothing happening. There can be no end to a thing that never started.

Once you know what your book is about and what happens in it, at least in general, you are in a position to find your first scene. The first scene will contain the moment in the "time" of your fiction in which the happening, the action, becomes sufficiently inevitable to put the writing into motion and aim it down the right path. The right path is the path into *what* happens and *how* what happens ends.

Knowing what happens in your book will also enable you to determine what the final scene should be, because once what is to happen in the book has *happened,* you stop. You stop! No epilogues, no postmortems.

Like the magnificent Frost essay on the dynamics of a poem—"like a piece of ice on a hot stove the poem must ride on its own melting"—a work of fiction consumes its own materials. Make sure it does or you will suffer the fate of Sisyphus.

The fiction writer must select his scenes with the utmost care because any work of fiction is an act of enormous compression and condensation. No novel is ever "true to life." No story either. Its truths and its effects are those of seeming, not of fact—if fact is ever ascertainable. The writer is, if you like, rationed as to words and pages with which to put this semblance of reality into dramatic form.

I don't presume here to try to teach anyone how to select a scene. There are certain kinds of scenes that cannot be written by a particular writer, and he has to find a new way of saying what he wants to say. I don't think anyone could teach Jane Austen how to write a thunderously huge scene like one of Thomas Mann's in *The Magic Mountain*. I don't think it could be done. No one would want to either, but the point is that every writer has to work within the frame of his own material. For the beginning writer, it is important to select scenes that he can handle. If yours is an historical novel try not to have a log cabin raising unless you know how they were actually built. Do not attempt scenes of madness unless you know what you are talking about—it is fascinating to speculate who "sat" for King Lear.

Even more important, the writer must know exactly what each scene accomplishes in and for the novel. Whether or not any one scene can be called "obligatory," nothing in a novel can exist unrelated to the rest. No scene can be put into a novel, and read by the reader, without coloring the reader's mind from that point on to the end; all the preceding scenes are the parents and ancestors of the next one. The experience of fiction is accumulative as well as sequential. All scenes are contributory and all scenes are contributory on most of the various levels of the novel. List, if you must, what each scene does for the action, for the characterizations, for the foreshadowing, for the reader's entire experience of your fiction. Lay the scenes out in front of you and look at them in as relaxed a way as you can and see what they say back to you. But keep in mind that a scene that shows the reader nothing except a couple of characters being all too forgettable is not a scene but a fictional entry.

Scenes are something like miniature stories. They have in them the germ of the entire story or book, and they are like the larger whole in other respects. Scenes have a beginning and an ending, like any complete story. Each scene has a means of perception. Occasionally more than one, but rarely. Each scene has a setting—it takes place somewhere. Each scene poses the same problems that the story or novel poses. It must establish the reader as fast as possible. It must give evidence as soon as possible that it intends to continue the contract with the reader.

Scenes are constructed as invisibly as possible, just as the entire novel or short story is constructed. As with the first and last scene, every single scene commences, after the writer has selected or "found" the scene, at the moment when it becomes necessary to the action of the story. The scene ends when its point has been made, even though the characters are still talking their heads off. It is the death of good scene writing to add anticlimactic material.

Scenes need to be economical and even spare in their construction. No characters not germane to the purpose of the scene should be permitted on stage. No information for its own quaint sake should be included as window dressing: "It was a lovely old spoon which had come to her years ago from Aunt Martha's estate." This is all right if the spoon with its genealogy is necessary to project character or action or whatever, and is not just something with which tea is being stirred.

Scenes move in terms of action, of character change and development, in terms of the passage of time—a sunken sub with the air running out, the ticking clock, so favorite a dramatic device, a symbol in itself of motion and consumption—and above all, in a rather mysterious fashion, they derive much of their motion from the reader. This last is something like the learning process and we know little about it except that the reader experiences a sense of accumulation, of growth as he is reading.

Scenes have a lot of work to do. Not only do they have to advance the work of fiction in terms of action, character, and theme, but they require a solution to the problem of transitions. These fictional scene dividers may be of an infinite variety and should, of course, be made as inconspicuous as possible. When transitions become an integral part of the action they do many things. They show the passage of time: "Three hours later we were still at it." They interpret the setting as part of the action: "The big room, when she entered, was being made ready for the solemn occasion." They even characterize: "In his usual aimless fashion he had neglected to provide for their arrival." Scenes can be constructed so that no transition is needed. If the reader can find his way quickly enough into the new scene he will have made his own transition.

There is, of course, no prescription for the number of scenes in a novel or a story. The freedom of fiction is to be its own length. Some short stories, especially very short ones, may comprise only a single scene, though the singleness is often more apparent than actual. Most modern novels use a great many scenes, particularly when the cast of characters is large. Varying the length of the scenes and the number of characters in them will avoid monotony. It is fatally easy to fall into the trap of two-character scenes, one after another.

In the passage from Henry James cited earlier, to him, apparently, the number of possible scenes in a novel is as nearly infinite as the holes in a huge canvas, the canvas of life itself. He is right about that, obviously so. But first you have to see the canvas, and then you have to notice the holes, and then you have to plan the embroidery, select the holes needed for the pattern, thread the needle, and commence. The trouble with most new writers is that the whole canvas is not there, by implication, and there isn't much variety in the threads. The new writer also tends to lean too heavily on his favorite colors, to miss some holes and put too much thread through some of the others, creating bumps. Even worse, some will have borrowed their patterns, and not enough of them will have gone to look at the Gobelins and the fabrics of Peru and Byzantium.

Every year I receive one or more manuscripts that are not written in scenes. With some exceptions they bear certain marks of kinship, one with another. They contain numerous prose essays and explanation, which in nonfiction would not be interesting or accurate enough. There is a great deal of interior monologue by the central character. And in general they read like thinly disguised autobiography. This is not meant condescendingly. What I mean is that the avoidance of scene usually indicates fictional material insufficiently digested, a piece of writing begun before it had been sufficiently ruminated.

To use an example available to everyone, in Fitzgerald's young autobiographical novel, *This Side of Paradise,* the fictional continuum lapses into scene, frequently in fragments of dialogue, rather than develops into scene. These lapses most often occur when a confrontation is needed. Confrontations are difficult to the point of impossibility in a fictional continuum treatment.

Thus far I have not discussed this notion of confrontation. In the selection of scenes, I believe it to be a prime consideration. By confrontation I mean a meeting between apparently incompatible elements: two armies, two kinds of love, good and evil, fire and flood, pilot and storm, mongoose and snake, parent and child, cops and robbers, honor and treachery, money and need—the list is as large as mankind has managed to become old. My reading of unsuccessful manuscripts proves nothing, but it suggests that this element of confrontation is the heart of almost all good scenes. Even in scenes of anguish with a single character, there is the Devil in opposition. The confrontation has to be felt, or experienced, in each scene directly by the character with whom the reader is identifying himself, but also shown to be felt by the other party or parties to it.

The entire matter of the story of the Good Samaritan takes place between Jesus and the lawyer in thirteen verses of St. Luke's account, but it will repay any fiction writer's prolonged study.

And, behold, a certain lawyer stood up, and tempted him, saying, Master, what shall I do to inherit eternal life?

He said unto him, What is written in the law? how readest thou?

And he answering said, Thou shalt love the Lord thy God with all thy heart, and with all thy soul, and with all thy strength, and with all thy mind; and thy neighbour as thyself.

Scene

And he said unto him, Thou hast answered right: this do, and thou shalt live.

But he, willing to justify himself, said unto Jesus, And who is my neighbour?

And Jesus answering said, A certain man went down from Jerusalem to Jericho, and fell among thieves, which stripped him of his raiment, and wounded him, and departed, leaving him half dead.

And by chance there came down a certain priest that way: and when he saw him, he passed by on the other side.

And likewise a Levite, when he was at the place, came and looked on him, and passed on the other side.

But a certain Samaritan, as he journeyed, came where he was: and when he saw him, he had compassion on him.

And went to him, and bound up his wounds, pouring in oil and wine, and set him on his own beast, and brought him to an inn, and took care of him.

And on the morrow when he departed, he took out two pence, and gave them to the host, and said unto him, Take care of him; and whatever thou spendest more, when I come again, I will repay thee.

Which now of these three, thinkest thou, was neighbour unto him that fell among the thieves?

And he said, He that showed mercy on him. Then said Jesus unto him, Go, and do thou likewise.

Notice that there is no plot, as such, only a confrontation, but what a confrontation! Though extremely short, this story of Jesus and the agent-provocateur lawyer consists of two scenes, one framing the other. Yet if you think of the St. Luke Gospel as a work of fiction about a religious leader destroyed by the society he feels impelled to save, consider some of the dividends from this scene-within-a-scene: a fore-shadowing of the end of Jesus' ministry; a terrific intensification of the irony of the execution of Jesus; a superb, brief, incisive addition to the characterization of Jesus; the lawyer as a reflection of the establishment; society as a member of the cast (men put Jesus to death). It is really unnecessary to elaborate further upon this particular demonstration of the power of the scene, except to remark that everything the scene means is right in there, and nothing else is.

Six

FICTION IS PEOPLE

After everything else has been said and proposed about fiction, the fact remains that it is not only *for* people, but it is made up *of* people, and everything in a work of fiction is there because it was put there by a person—the writer.

People—characters—are the true substance of all fiction, most nonfiction, all drama, and a lot of poetry ranging from the *Iliad* to Robert Lowell. It is the great gallery of people in the Bible who stand for characters in all later European writing, and next to the Bible, Shakespeare. Adam, Eve, Cain, Abel, David, Saul, Ruth, Job, Jonah, Elijah, Jacob, Moses, Pharoah, Pontius Pilate, Judas, the list is infinitely long. My point is that the Bible and its lessons are remembered as the stories of people.

People are not the principal subject of fiction; they are its only subject. Kipling's ship that found herself is not a ship but a human character, a female human character in a particular time and place. Maria, in *Storm,* by George Stewart, like her sisters before and after, is a storm, but a personified storm, a goddess out of the eternal pantheon of the weather.

> As from the union of two opposite germ-cells begins a life, so from the contact of northern and southern air had sprung something which before had not been. As a new life, a focus of activity, begins to develop after its kind and grow strong by what it feeds on, so in the air that complex of forces began to develop and grow strong. A new storm had begun.

There is no such entity as a piece of fiction that is devoid of human beings or personifications; by the nature of ourselves and our lives there cannot be any such fiction. People *are* the story and the whole story.

The reader reads fiction more for its people than for any other element, whether plot, setting, or shock value. Readers associate characters in fiction with their own lives and with their own experience. They will even name their children after fictional characters. If you name a child after a character in a book, you are saying something about that character and also about your relationship to that piece of reading. Characters from great pieces of fiction have become symbolic types in our language and in other languages. We are all familiar with Hamlet, Camille, Galahad, the Ugly American, Gatsby, Shylock, Lucky Jim, Captain Queeg, and Griselda, to name a few. People accept great characters into their vocabularies in the same way that they accept great figures of history and great entertainers. They equate fictional characters with actual people, living and dead. No matter what the novelist begins with—an abstract idea, an enterprise, war, country, a physical feat, a single object, flower, portrait, house, or whatever—it becomes fiction only by virtue of its characters. The novel *is* the people that are in it. Slavery in the antebellum South is a subject, but in the hands of Harriet Beecher Stowe slavery is Uncle Tom and Little Eva. The ramifications of this obvious fact could occupy all the pages of a much longer chapter than this one. Such writing problems as the selection of characters and the naming of them are intricate indeed.

Perhaps the most central matter to the inexpert writer is the apparent temptation to try to use real people in his fiction. This is not the reality of the problem because no writer can or does use real people. He does not even know himself fully, and all he knows about other people is what he has observed and felt about them himself. That is why, for example, there is really no such thing as a "definitive" biography, or an impartial one. By the same token there is no such thing as a complete autobiography, either. The *Reader's Digest*'s "The Most Unforgettable Character I Ever Met" says it well. The gist of this title is wholly subjective, not only in the case of the words "unforgettable" and "I," but in the case of almost every other word. "Most" is a writer's judgment. So is "character," since it has a special and qualitative meaning, or more than one, to each of us. It is hopeless to try to put another person on paper when all you have to work with is your own impression of that person. So, all fictional and nonfictional characters have to begin by being subjective to you, the writer.

A second temptation the beginning writer must avoid is to invent characters to solve large or small fictional problems. There is an ancient term for this kind of character—deus ex machina—in connection with exigencies arising out of unmanageable plots. But there are other invented characters—ones thrown in for the purpose of authenticity—the simple, philosophical fisherman, or the taxi driver who knows all the answers, or the flamboyant aunt who is supposed to make the reader laugh, or the sophisticate designed to make the writer appear so. Any and all of these and many more like them are nothing but set pieces. Mere character for its own sake is not unforgettable, it is irritating. If a character in a novel or a story is a "character" that must be a part of the action. Otherwise the writer is wasting the reader's time in a self-seeking display of versatility. Remember that consciously or subconsciously, the reader has put his trust in you and expects all the characters to be necessary. Characters are sometimes brought into a novel just for the sake of the crowd, as a part of the setting. Even a low-grade sociologist does not make this mistake. So, one of the primary rules about characters in fiction is that all of them must contribute to the narrative motion.

A third, less obvious danger is the static character, the one who is the same at the end of the novel as at the beginning. This is a difficult point. One way of putting it would be to say that the same characters who appear in scene one and scene thirty must be different enough so that the scenes

Fiction is People

would not come out as they do if the order were transposed. People grow. Characters grow like people. They change for all the human reasons—hate, fear, age, health—anything. The same soldier thinks one way about battle before he is in love, and another, different way after he has fallen in love. A woman loves a man differently before she has children. These human interactions are crucial to the development of any kind of novel except the very crudest. It does not matter whether it is essentially a novel of plot or of theme.

Editor's note: From a letter, February 7, 1960, to Richard Wormser:

> This business of building character is in some ways the toughest part of long fiction writing, and it is one of the points where, it seems to me, a good novel differs most markedly from a good short story. In a novel, growth and change in a character are part of the forward narrative motion of the book.

A character is never a whole person, but just those parts of him that fit the story or the piece of writing. So the act of selection is the writer's first step in delineating character. From what does he select? From a whole mass of what Bernard DeVoto used to call, somewhat clinically, "placental material." He must know an enormous amount more about each of his characters than he will ever use directly—childhood, family background, religion, schooling, health, wealth, sexuality, reading, tastes, hobbies—an endless questionnaire for the writer to fill out. For example, the writer knows that people speak, and therefore his characters will describe themselves indirectly when they talk. Clothing is a means of characterization. In short, each character has a style of his own in everything he does. These need not all be listed, but the writer should have a sure grasp of them. If he has, his characters will, within the book, read like people.

Editor's note: From a letter, October 14, 1947, to Ernest K. Gann:

> As for this business of my insisting on knowing too much . . . I must state again, as I told you before, that whatever appears in this book, what doesn't appear in it is like the underwater part of an iceberg. You ought to know just about everything about your characters. There is nothing about them that you will find superfluous in writing the book with them in it. If you know everything about your characters, then you will always succeed in visualizing them for the reader in one way or another, even if you never resort to a descriptive sentence. But there are plenty of places in your manuscript where you have just written along, inventing enough about the person in question to carry the story, and this, my friend, is second-rate writing.

Sexuality is one aspect of characterization. I could say "sex," but that would suggest action, and I think that sex in fiction is too often mistaken for direct and explicit action. All living organisms have sexuality, since all perpetuate themselves, and most of them reproduce themselves. It is obvious that all characters in fiction have sexuality. The writer must know about his characters' sexualities, and about the many ways of handling them. In Kipling, for example, sex is always or almost always offstage and viewed mythically or tribally or biologically. But in much fiction the sexual behavior of the characters is one of the central elements of the book, as in *Madame Bovary* and *Lady Chatterley's Lover* and *Lolita.* Sex, used by such authors, is always illustrated and presented in terms of its effects and its causes, and not, in a kind of reverse, cheerful, pornographic innocence, for its own sake, as in *Fanny Hill.* Sex in a novel is no substitute for emotion.

Editor's note: From a letter, October 19, 1949, to Ernest K. Gann:

> I am now going to give you hell about the final six pages of this manuscript. I concede, to begin with, that Bruno is bound to be thinking with almost frenzied hunger about Connie and Connie's body and sleeping with Connie and so on, but I submit that the middle of page 243 is a great deal more explicit than it needs to be. Actually, of course, Bruno would be thinking partly in such bald terms; but, Ernie, a substantial fraction of the adult population of this country has enjoyed the act of sexual intercourse one or more times and they are fairly familiar with the mechanics of it. Worse than that, so detailed a description results, in the case of this particular reader, in thinking more about copulation than about your book, and this, frankly, I don't want.

From this catalogue of personal and social facts about his characters, the writer selects those elements that build the novel and make it inevitable: cowardice or courage, passion, miserliness, sense of inferiority, or whatever, and he leaves out all the material that is not relevant to the structure and content of his fiction. Sometimes this works a hardship on a writer who has done his homework. Once he has begun to shape a character, he can invent almost endlessly, and it seems a pity to waste the invention. But it is not wasted. If this richness is there, it will show in everything the character does and says and thinks, implicitly.

Characterization is close to the core of the reader's illusion. In drama the writer creates a character who is interpreted by the actor. The role is the generalization of the specific character. Hence the many Hamlets or Lears or Juliets. The possibility exists that the fiction writer also writes roles and the reader supplies the actors. The character that is rendered too meticulously often fails to convince. Too little is left for the reader to contribute out of himself. General physical descriptions are usually enough; the reader will supply his own visual image and because it is his own it will be a reality for him. How often we hear somebody say, "Oh, I pictured her entirely differently." I venture to suggest that this is why using people from real life seldom succeeds in fiction. The real life person is just that one person, and that person is never the reader. If there is any success, it is a biographical one at best, and hence nonfiction. So, characters are not found or copied or noted down. They are, in effect, translated by the writer's imagination. Each character is a piece of the writer and the writer's experience of other human beings, and also a piece of the reader and the reader's parallel experience.

Fiction is People

The writer's imagination must also translate the speech of his characters, the people of his novel. Like real people, they talk. But they are not real people and their talk cannot be transcriptions of real talk. There is not room enough in a novel for the way people really talk. Proof of this is to be found by leaving a tape recorder on during the course of a party at home. The basic difference between the random taped conversation and what the writer must do is condensation by selectivity. Hemingway has overproved this. Like characters and their delineation, dialogue presents many problems. Some are easy to avoid, but others are harder to detect when the writer comes to edit his own manuscripts.

To confuse a novel with a play—which is obstensibly dialogue—is to mistake the nature of the media, but turn for a moment to a comparison with the theater. Dialogue in theater is revised in rehearsal until it comes easily to the player in the part. This is commendable. Try reading your own dialogue aloud sometimes to see if it is sayable. Dialogue in theater is the principal means of advancing the action. It ought to be a major means of advancing the action in the novel and too often isn't. Dialogue in theater is not so important a means of characterization as in fiction because of the physical presence of the actor. In fiction it is a primary tool for delineating character.

In his "Prologue" to *Sweet Thursday,* one of Steinbeck's characters says:

> Well, I like a lot of talk in a book, and I don't like to have nobody tell me what the guy that's talking looks like. I want to figure out what he looks like from the way he talks. And

another thing—I kind of like to figure out what the guy's thinking by what he says.

Dialogue does many other things: it describes setting, develops conflict, depicts change, foreshadows what is to come, and reminds of what is past. It is a chief means of exposition and even a method of transition. In short, it does everything that characterization and the other fused parts of a novel do and in a good novel all these are often going on at once.

Dialogue is easier to handle if there is a means of perception. This is tremendously important in scenes with a lot of characters on stage. The author of course has to do all the talking, but the reader "hears" it better when it reaches him through a central perceiver.

But dialogue cannot carry the whole burden as it does in a play. If it could we could learn about government from reading the Congressional Record. There is, however, a tentative rule that pertains to all fiction dialogue. It must do more than one thing at a time or it is too inert for the purposes of fiction. This may sound harsh, but I consider it an essential discipline.

Let's begin with dialogue as characterization. One common error with new writers is static dialogue. Writers guilty of this fault are aware that people talk, so they invent characters that talk, too. But these characters are dull talkers. They do not say anything. They do not talk to the point of the book. They talk in orderly rote, like a panel. They always use the same vocabulary no matter to whom they are talking. And since they have no tone of voice of their own, you can't tell who is talking.

Each and every character must have his or her own vocabulary. The personal nature of vocabularies is as distinctive as fingerprints, but in a bad novel all the characters seem to use the same one. Furthermore, all too frequently, it is the author's own way of talking. This results in monotony as well as in the reader's confusion. To offset that, the author uses a whole string of identifiers: "Geraldine simpered," "Hans thundered," "Pierre insinuated leeringly," "Teddy gulped," "Irene hissed," and so on. So, what have we here? A violation of the means of perception rule. All those verbs of identification and characterization are the author talking. "Said" is better than any of them. No writer should be afraid of overworking this simple verb. Indirect identification is best of all: "The smile left his face abruptly. 'I don't like the sound of that' " [he said].

Every character, like every person, has more than one vocabulary. Children seem to have at least two. A convict talks one way to his mother, another way to his girl or to the warden or to a fellow inmate. A woman tells the same thing differently to a man and to another woman. The author needs to know about each of his characters where he got his vocabulary, and to select the words his character uses from the company he is keeping. This is a good and subtle effect for both characterization and the advancement of action.

Editor's note: From a letter to Richard Wormser, February 14, 1960:

This is a scene with three characters, and the dialog has to be most carefully checked to maintain the differences among them. . . . At the top of the page, you have Moses talking a good deal like Young. One writing device that might be useful to you in handling Moses is to be familiar with Mormon hymns, which intoxicated Moses, and have his speech move to the same rhythms—by which I do not mean singsongy.

Novels and stories take place in settings. In Shakespeare's theater the actors described the scene: "Well, this is the forest of Arden." Or, "How sweet the moonlight looks upon this bank." But in fiction, where there is nothing exterior for the reader to look at, the attempt to set scene and develop setting by spoken description is failure and makes all characters sound alike. Many opportunities can be found for getting around this. Two brief lines of dialogue can picture a room and characterize the speakers at the same time:

"And this, Jessie, is my Louis Quatorze dining room."
"Oh, my dear, what makes you think so?"

A whole landscape can be shown in terms of a direction giving or a warning. This also permits foreshadowing and transition. A.B. Guthrie tells us a good deal about the landscape and also characterizes the speakers in this passage from *The Way West:*

The lead wagons were sinking from sight down a slope that Rebecca figured led to the Laramie. It was as if the wheels were sinking into the earth pair by pair, and then the beds and then the swaying tops.

Lije whoaed his oxen when he came to the top of the hill. Rebecca walked up to him and saw the train winding down and, below it, Fort Laramie, white as fresh wash, with trees waving and shade dark on the grass and the river fringed with woods. More to herself than to Lije she said, "I never thought to be so glad just to see a building."

"It's Fort Laramie. Sure."

"Not because it's a fort. Just because it's a building."

"It's Fort Laramie all the same."

"You reckon they've got chairs there, Lije? Real chairs."

There was light in his eyes. He said, "Sure," and cut a little caper with his feet and sang out:

"To the far-off Pacific sea,
Will you go, will you go, old girl, with me?"

She said, "I just want to set in a chair."

The words the characters speak are spoken to other characters. The principle of selectivity means that the element of sparring, almost the idea of attack and defense, is needed to make dialogue advance the action. Know what the scene is supposed to accomplish and have your characters talk toward it, not in circles.

Dialogue depicts change:

"No man says a thing like that to a woman," she said finally, "unless he hates her."

"Or unless he is beginning to love her."

Dialogue reminds of what is past. Often novels have dialogue that exists in the absence of all that preceded the scene.

Let your characters refer to their own pasts as characters in the novel, as Somerset Maugham does in *The Moon and Sixpence:*

> "I was not fifteen when my father found that I had a lover," she said. "He was third mate on the *Tropic Bird*. A good-looking boy."
>
> She sighed a little. They say a woman always remembers her first lover with affection; but perhaps she does not always remember him.
>
> "My father was a sensible man."
>
> "What did he do?" I asked.
>
> "He thrashed me within an inch of my life, and then he made me marry Captain Johnson. I did not mind. He was older, of course, but he was good-looking too."

Dialogue expresses theme. A character in the book talks about what the book is about, as if by inadvertence informing the reader no less than the character listening. The easy illustration to pick here is the great drunken speech of Greenwald's in *The Caine Mutiny*. This is a real use of dialogue not only as theme but as rhetoric. Yet every successful novel is likely to have its essential theme expressed in dialogue. This expression must come from one character who is in character, and be directed toward another character. Never toward the reader.

More than words enters into the problem of dialogue. What is *not* said as well as what *is* matters. Here the operative principle is again selectivity. Choice includes and excludes. Nothing should be said that is not germane to the entire novel. In terms of the pitfalls: no witty remarks because the author, not the reader or the character, thinks they are witty. No excessive use of dialect, the use of an argot for its own sake. No character revealing himself by expounding a philosophy of life merely to show how he feels about the world in general, but only to express feelings about the world of the book. The poor country cousin of the philosophy of life is the comment on life of the Thackeray sort. Eschew these on behalf of all characters *unless* they advance the action as well as characterize the speaker.

Editor's note: From a letter to Robert Gold, June 28, 1965:

> The sample of the dialog you sent along in the middle section of your letter is interesting and while I just can't today and at this late hour say very much about the use of dialect and fiction dialog, I will say I am still of the same opinion that I have been, on the numerous occasions when I and others lectured at Bread Loaf. Don't overdo it typographically. The whole idea is not to duplicate a dialect but to suggest it. If you don't believe me, go to the nearest public library and take out Joel Chandler Harris's *Uncle Remus* and try reading it aloud to somebody.

Dialogue treated as spoken speech is not the only kind of dialogue. Indirect discourse is another. In very skillful hands, even the narration of events can become a dialogue of its own. William Golding's *The Inheritors* is an example. Here the author had to invent everything, including an unguessable language, which grew out of an unguessable and never known kind of subhuman being. Much of the dialogue in it is not direct in essence but rather a translation. The same could be said of Tolkien's *Lord of the Rings*.

Finally, there is the interior monologue. Hemingway employs this device throughout *For Whom The Bell Tolls* as a means of characterizing Robert Jordan and of foreshadowing the end. But there is a potential danger in its use.

Editor's note: From a letter to Richard Wormser, February 21, 1960:

> Page 48: 5th line—"like someone had, etc." If this is Ned's interior thought the grammar is perhaps all right, but it is wrong for English. This brings me to the point that it is better to characterize in interior monolog without dialect or fractured grammar—dialect in an interior monolog is a contradiction in psychological terms.

Wormser disagreed, saying he thought that all characters should think within their own vocabulary. In his next letter, March 20, W.S. answered as follows:

> Page 3: Below middle: "He'd kind of like to see that." This is a trick of inner dialog that you tend to use a lot of times, and often I don't find it wholly successful. . . . As for your point about interior dialog, we could correspond for a long time about this. First of all, there are about a dozen voices talking inside us all the time. Man dreams, waking or sleeping, from birth, and perhaps before, to death and possibly after. Some of the voices are almost mythically old. Some are not voices at all but pictures. Not even the greatest

Fiction is People

writers have been able to do justice to this, but in terms of the kind of novel we have here, it is important that the *substance* of the interior monologs be consonant with the facets of the various characters which the writer displays in the course of his story. He cannot display the whole.

It is certainly more popular to tell you that there are no principles, no dos and don'ts, in this and the other areas of fiction writing. You are free to let talent override deficiencies of technique, and this is exactly what happens, *always,* in the work of great writers. Sufficient virtue will indeed cover a multitude of sins. Techniques like the ones I have discussed here are not essential if your talent permits you to disregard them. But the technical faults of great writers do not give carte blanche to do likewise. Be a master of theme and you will be forgiven a limping structure. Be a great social novelist like Thackeray and you can lecture your reader and point a moral if you think it adorns your tale. But great novelists, or even entertaining novelists, are so by reason of their strengths. A novelist like James Gould Cozzens can create worlds in book after book in which there are no children and no really convincing women, and get away with it. He cannot successfully characterize women, and he cannot put women's words into their mouths and produce the effect of women talking together.

Seven

ON KNOWING
YOUR MATERIAL

A vital aspect of the fiction-writing process, and most surely of all creative writing processes, is the matter of density. By density I mean richness, substance. It is the core of knowing your materials.

Density is one of the most difficult aspects of fiction to discuss because it is not a separate element like plot or even characterization. Rather it is a part of everything else. Real density is achieved when the optimum number of things is going on at once, some of them overtly, others by implication.

Writing is not a matter of a single, simple progression, with each sentence making only one point. Every paragraph, every sentence is related to the entire rest of the book, and if it is not so related it is superfluous. By "the entire rest of of the book" I mean what is to come as well as what has gone before. The part of the book already read is stored in the reader's memory bank, and each new word is added to that storehouse. But in many ways what is being read is an invisible prophecy of what is to come. This is one part of the ingredient of density. There are many others.

A good piece of fiction is something like the Scot's definition of the haggis: "A deal o' fine confoosed feeding." All parts of each scene are working: characterization of the people portrayed, creation of the physical world of the story, narrative motion, whetting of anticipation, resolution of the mystery, characterization of the author—style inevitably does this—all the dimensions and all at once.

The enemy of fictional density is the one-thing-at-a-time scene, that simply shows you, the reader, one of the facets of the story, whether it be something about the characters or about the action or the setting, or whatever. All too often this thin scene is invented to convey a piece of factual information to the reader—a tea party where the characters talk about their ancestors and their families, and, perhaps, as an added fictional bit of icing on the cake, announce that a new teacher is coming to town.

Fiction writers are limited as to words. A novelist generally has between 75,000 and 150,000 words in all within which to give the reader a gamut of experience that would, if he were to try to tell it all in detail, require millions. If the writer manages the feat, he will have achieved a lot of density. It could be said that James Joyce accomplished this in *Ulysses,* which takes place in the space of one day.

So, the overwhelmingly obvious fact about what a writer does when he sets down a story is that he selects. On what basis? Clearly, selection has to be made on the basis of appropriateness, but that still leaves a vast lumberyard. Perhaps, too, selection is influenced by the author's ability to control his material. Mostly, though, the criterion is probably something like "function." The fiction writer chooses what will "work" for him, what will advance his work in progress. He chooses against the book he is trying to write, the feeling he is trying to convey. It's not the critical elements of which the book is composed, but its content, its deepest theme, the whole thing in potential that exists in him. From one word he chooses to the next word, and from one sentence to the next sentence, and from scene to scene. And sometimes he chooses without pause and sometimes he has to sit and think a long time.

This process of selection by the novelist gives the literary critic a hundred different approaches to his work. Whenever a novelist elects, selects something, he generally leaves a small trace of one or two of his other available choices, and this permits a multiple discussion of any work of fiction, which keeps at least academic criticism alive for a century if properly exposed.

The intention here is to stress the choices of the novelist. The bulk of writing goes on in his head before anything is put on paper. The mind proposes or confects something. Then, at least in my case, there is a sort of galloping off with roads constantly diverging. Usually a partial dead end before another foray. There is no going back in a novel. Once something is given to the reader, the author is bound by it.

This necessary and constant process of selection, of choice, is not enough by itself. Because novels are so compressed, allusory, so made up of token material and not entire reality, every word, every scene has to function as more than just itself. A scene does not merely depend on what has preceded it; the scene also enlarges that preceding by showing what resulted from it. Until, indeed, the end is in the beginning. Once the scene has been selected, the writer needs to ask himself some questions about it. How does it move the narration forward? Where and how does it begin and end? Who is to be the means of perception? Who are the necessary characters in the scene? How is the characterization being enriched, deepened in the reader's mind, the physical world of the novel—time, place, setting—expanded and affirmed, the theme of the novel enriched? How does the scene interpret preceding scenes and remind the reader of them inconspicuously, or conspicuously? How does it foreshadow the next scene, or the rest of the book?

By the same token, all dialogue continuously characterizes the speaker and retains the means of perception. Sometimes establishes the setting. Builds conflict, foreshadows, expounds.

Settings, too. What would *The Magic Mountain* and *Death in Venice* be like without their settings? Main Street, Zenith, Harrisburg, Pa., Yoknapatawpha County, Schofield Barracks, and so on and on. These places are not scenery for its own sake. They are central parts of the stories their writers laid in them. Settings affect the action and the mood, they change the characters. Try *Lord Jim* for some of that. Not to mention *Wuthering Heights*.

The number of characters is also an index to length and narrative complexity. *Deliverance* is an all-male cast and a small one. The size of the setting also defines the fictional

On Knowing Your Material

dimension. *War and Peace* is set in a continent—the largest continent—and its cast of characters, onstage and implied, numbers in the millions and includes whole nations and peoples.

The writer's fictional intention determines the dimension. He selects the right-sized piece for giving the reader the experience of what happens and to whom. He must know all the options. Adding things on will not increase the stature. If you increase your cast of characters, what happens in your fiction must be relevant to all of them or else they are supernumeraries. And a novel is not the Metropolitan Opera with its chorus of spear carriers. Nor will placing the action in a vast plain surrounded by snow-capped mountains make the story majestic.

Editor's note: From a letter, August 3, 1960, to Allen Drury:

I was impressed in *Advise* with your settings and "furniture," so to speak. Your rooms and houses and gardens and roads are all used to further the action of the book—they are never "set pieces" which so often mar amateur writing. Also, you use your setting to affect your characters as well as influence them. And, in a broader sense, your setting is Government, and you, like Cozzens and a few other contemporary novelists, know how much a great institution becomes a part of the people connected with it.

While it is true that character makes the action, in a good novel the action also changes and makes the character. This is what is wrong with "Gunsmoke" and "Bonanza" and

"The Doctors" and the rest of the television serials we have all grown older watching. Although secondary characters in a "Mr. Novak" or a "Kojak" may be changed by what happens in the script, the main ones have to remain reliably the same. Matt Dillon and Ironside may put on some weight around the middle, but they do not change inside. Even in an action novel like *The Guns of Navarone,* the way in which events in their turn change and make the characters is one of the excitements.

Density is the opposite of thinness. In its nature it is not divisible. It is not made by lamination but by fusion. It is always there, any place at all in the book. An editor can open a manuscript to any page and tell its presence or absence. In Hemingway's scene of the retreat from Caporetto in *A Farewell To Arms,* the line "They said to me, 'Who's dead next, Tenente? Where do we go from here?'" characterizes the speakers, characterizes the hero who hears it, characterizes me, the reader, and foreshadows the whole tragic romance of the book.

This omnipresent quality of successful fiction is extremely easy to recognize once you have learned to look for it. In order to see it in all its complexity, you might reread some books that you've read recently. Reread while the whole book is sharply present in your mind. See how you become aware of the fusion and the density.

When it comes to your own writing, the quality of density will take time to achieve. I believe that it is most likely to result from a lot of prewriting rumination. Telling the novel over, piecemeal, in your mind. Rubbing one part against another until the foreground section has been "tumbled"

On Knowing Your Material

against the other sections. It is no use writing some parts of a novel in order to get to "other parts" or climaxes. Every sentence, every line of dialogue is important. At some instant, that is the sentence or the speech that the reader will be reading. If the narrative is in motion, it must contain everything needful and nothing for its own separate sake.

A writer has a lot of material from which to choose and the fitting together progressively of all his writing choices is going gradually to give him a powerful momentum, and toward the end of the book he does not need to go into something at great length again. Once he has found the setting, for example—selected the setting—that matches the scene, he does not have to show it all over again chapter by chapter and scene by scene and close the curtains more than once in the room. He can rely on his selective process, which becomes at once more difficult and easier as he goes along. He doesn't ever make anything up. He searches until he finds it.

Now this is very, very hard interior work, and there is no such thing as instant fiction. The work goes on all the time; while you're driving your car, while you're brushing your teeth, when you're falling asleep, when you're waking up. It's going on inside you all the time. Constantly, that's where all the writing is done, except the setting down of it. And to dodge this enormously difficult work is to be lazy, and to be lazy is to be dull. To be dull is to be unread. And it's as simple a progression as that.

At Bread Loaf alone, and without counting my professional experience elsewhere, I have read over five-hundred manuscripts. Yet, looking back, I cannot recall a single one of them that was intrinsically boring or hopeless. Every one was about some part of the human experience, and mankind is not bored with being man. It is bored by individual people who are bores, but *not* with the experience of life. So I would tell a writer not to worry about the potential of his material. He's only got one kind and that's exactly the same as everybody who went before him had and everybody who comes after him will have, and that's himself and his fellow being, and it is surefire if properly handled. I don't suppose that anyone had a much narrower exposure to human material than a woman like Emily Dickinson, and it didn't seem somehow to result in any poverty of matter or manner or creativity on her part. The richness, the density is all there for any novelist. It is what he does when his sensibility is stirred that counts. It is what is selected and what is told. Sir Philip Sidney wrote, " 'Fool!' said my Muse to me, 'look in thy heart and write.' "

Writing fails because the writer does not know enough about his material. If he knows enough he will feel enough. The rest is editing, personal and otherwise. But any real writer does know enough. Every human being does. The difficulty is in knowing what you know. Unless you are discovering some things while engaged in this process of adjusting your material, you are probably not writing. Writing is not a typewriter, a piece of paper, and you. Writing is finding out what you really know, and knowing creates density.

One thing more: I urge those of you who are writing fiction to shun the impulse that diminishes the tension inside you while you are writing. Don't talk about your novel to

On Knowing Your Material

other people. Don't read sample sections to your Aunt Minnie or to your best friend or to anybody else. And then when you come back to it, when you're able to write, read over what you have written and see whether you yourself are bored to death by it or whether when the time comes that you reach the bottom of the last finished page, you say, "Give me another piece of paper."

Editor's note: From a letter, February 21, 1960, to Richard Wormser:

> You have a chance to end this scene on a strong note. Suppose there is a word from Brigham Young that the Mormons are still interested in Ned and Ned says that he has decided to work for the Army? Seems to me you can build the future conflict between Ned and the Mormons in such an interchange. . . . You haven't milked this scene anywhere near dry of what was actually going on . . . it's a crucial scene. Sides are being chosen up. You need to show this scene to the reader as strongly as you can, certainly with a great deal of underwriting. . . . Once again, give me more of all this—not more words but more *density*. Man, *be* Ned riding into Leavenworth. There are the Mormons. How would you feel if you were Ned?

Eight

THE NONFICTION WRITER

Nonfiction is the reading and writing mode of our time; in the broadest sense it is a mixture of art and education, of insight and information, without which we cannot live wise and informed lives. It is unfortunate that the term is so unsatisfactory. "Nonfiction" covers so wide a field that one could almost say it is writing that is *not* a number of things, rather than a genre of its own. Thus, an entry in the *Encyclopaedia Britannica* is nonfiction, but so is the label on a tin can, a book review, a newspaper editorial, a how-to-do-it book or article, a political pamphlet (at least it is allegedly nonfiction), a work of history (which is an art or a science depending on what university you attended), a masterpiece of rhetoric like the Gettysburg Address, a monograph on the Osmanli Turks, the Department of Agriculture Yearbook, and the annual report of American Telephone & Telegraph.

In some quarters there is the notion that nonfiction is supposed to be didactic—to teach its reader something, tell him a message for his own good, inform his untutored mind. In other words, nonfiction may be dimly associated with textbooks, which are seldom really books at all. There is also a fairly general feeling that nonfiction is plebeian plaintalk of a sort easier to write than fiction or poetry because it can hobble along on the crutch of fact, or truth, which it does not have to "make up." Perhaps, but nothing is easier to write than bad writing; I have seen a bad poem written in less than five minutes. Dryden was right in calling prose "the other harmony." That harmony he speaks of can exist in nonfictional prose to the same extent that it does in fiction. Indeed, I suggest that some nonfiction is nearly indistinguishable from certain kinds and dimensions of fiction, that the reading delight can be as keen, and that the writing disciplines are closely comparable. It may seem absurd to compare qualitatively T. S. Eliot's "The Cocktail Party" and E. B. White's great essay, "The Death of a Pig," but in a profound sense both are about the same things. If fiction is *a* world, nonfiction is *the* world. In the end all writing is about the business of being human.

It could be said that nonfiction is written by two kinds of writers, who have two different motivations and belong to two different worlds. The first of these worlds is journalism, of course, and journalism practiced on a truly massive modern scale. It is marked by a relative immediacy of subject matter, a direct focus upon those six honest serving men of Kipling's, an attempt at communicating received information, and an often honorable attempt at interpretation.

The Nonfiction Writer

It may, and often does, concern itself with the instant present or the immediate future, as well as the recent past.

The second nonfictional world is that of scholarship. Here the ground rules are quite different. Scholarly writing begins in the graduate schools and its initial purpose is to prove the competence of the writer in his field. Unlike journalism, a lot of scholarly writing has almost no audience. It is likely to be read by an infinitesimal readership called by the author "my committee," and these few readers are hired and paid for in part to read what the graduate scholar has written. The emphasis is on visible competence in the field rather than on meaning to any reader. Whatever may be new, and hence potentially interesting, is apt to be hard to find. The proportion of discovery and novelty to the subject as a whole is that of a coral polyp to a barrier reef. The marshaling of evidence is the name of the game.

The lesser disciplines of spelling, punctuation, and grammar are not the distinction between these two kinds of writing. Nor, let me say at once, is the subject matter. There are no uninteresting subjects, only uninteresting writers. Any subject can also be made dull. The basic difference is the intention of the writing. Graduate school writing is defensive and self-seeking. Journalism, and I use the term in its highest sense, the sense in which even the Bible might be called God's Millennial Gazette, is an attempt to share, to communicate, to say something another person will understand. Both require research, of course, which may be as simple as checking facts or as intricate as working out the meanings of the two Hittite languages, but the purpose is different, the intentions usually dissimilar.

It is impossible to teach anyone *what* to write. The content must come from within. The importance of this short sentence cannot be exaggerated. All effective writing is about something, and almost all of it above the level of the soup can label, turns out to be about quite a lot of things fused or laced or linked together. Years ago an irreverent American author named Lucretia P. Hale, wrote a minor classic of American family life called *The Peterkin Papers*. The Peterkins were an impractical lot of well-meaning middle-class folk with a talent for self-defeat achieved by various forms of idiocy. The person who saved them from disaster was their neighbor, the Lady from Philadelphia. One day the Peterkins decided, as a family, that the oldest son, Solomon John, should be a writer. Accordingly they fitted out the attic room with a table, a ream of paper, a lot of sharp pencils, and a chair. Thither Solomon John repaired each morning after breakfast. Coming down only for meals, he spent days, weeks, a whole summer in the writer's attic.

When he finally descended the attic stairs for the last time the sheets of paper were still blank. He had written nothing because he could not think of anything to write about. The family was dismayed; as always in such crises they consulted the Lady from Philadelphia. She listened to their story with sympathy, smiled at Solomon John, and turning to the rest of the Peterkin family, observed, "Perhaps Solomon John is not a writer."

Perhaps not, indeed. But the disquieting thought persists that maybe Solomon John didn't *know* anything to write about. The first requirement of a writer is that he know something. The second requirement is not remarkably different. The wise writer writes about what he knows and *never* about what he knows nothing.

The nonfiction writer has two main approaches to his subject. One is through fresh information or experience, the other through fresh interpretation of the old. There isn't anything intrinsically new under the sun. The only newness of any kind is what man does with what's already there. This goes for astronomers no less than for writers and it is an obvious truth. Even so, everything changes. There is a need for the continuing re-relating of the past to bring its meaning to the immediate present. The more recondite the subject, the greater the necessity for so relating it.

No subject is so difficult as to require a large, special vocabulary. Some terms may be special, but the smaller the number the more effective the act of communication. A case in point is Rachel Carson's book, *The Silent Spring,* in which the author had to expound some highly technical matters without overt popularizing, and make the exposition stick against certain counterattack.

Practically no writing comes instantly out of the writer's head and down onto paper. Coleridge to the contrary. The road to Xanadu is a long road, and much of it goes on in the unconscious and subliminal mind. The first step for the nonfiction writer is to be sure, by turning it over in his mind, that his subject—if it is not assigned—is really what he wants to write about. This is done by a sort of mental digestion. After he has talked to himself about the writing until it begins to emerge, the writer prepares for the first draft by making notes. During this stage he keeps priming the pump by reading and exploring the subject, or the characters, or the implications of the future piece of writing. This is useful because it prevents his attempting to write on a subject in ignorance of what others may have done with it. If he knows what writers before him have said, he can avoid repetition of theme, style, usage. If possible, he tries to determine where the writing will end, and thus work back to the beginning. The beginning is the point at which he wishes the reader to become irrevocably involved with his subject.

Once the nonfiction writer has settled on his subject—what a writer has to write about—his next concern is words—what he has to write with. The nonfiction writer who is concerned with communication, not only to involve the reader but to honor the trust the reader places in him for accuracy, interest or entertainment, and interpretation, soon finds out that words are not to be taken for granted. And here I would like to comment on words as the editor sees them in the manuscripts that pass under his rarely delighted eye. I shall not dwell on the sweet uses of spelling and punctuation—though a reader relies on both—nor yet on the marvelous relationships between a virtue like clarity and the propositions, almost Euclidean, of grammar. The writer's problems with words, in the majority of these manuscripts, do not arise out of a vocabulary scarcity. The trouble arises, instead, out of not knowing the dictionary meanings of a word, exactly. The writer's meaning and the reader's meaning are determined by the use of the word, by its setting in the context of the rest of the piece of writing. A writer can stumble over spelling, be blind to etymologies, tone-deaf to sound and rhythm, but the essential matter is knowing the definition. It is quite likely that most people cannot define more than a tenth of the nouns and verbs that they habitually use.

In the marginal notes to his volume, *The Annotated Alice,* Martin Gardner writes, "If we wish to communicate accurately we are under a kind of moral obligation to avoid Humpty's practice of giving private meanings to commonly used words." The passage in *Alice* goes as follows:

"There's glory for you!"

"I don't know what you mean by 'glory,'" Alice said.

Humpty Dumpty smiled contemptuously. "Of course you don't—till I tell you. I meant 'there's a nice knock-down argument for you!'"

"But 'glory' doesn't mean 'a nice knock-down argument,'" Alice objected.

"When *I* use a word," Humpty Dumpty said, in rather a scornful tone, "it means just what I choose it to mean—neither more nor less."

"The question is," said Alice, "whether you *can* make words mean so many different things."

"The question is," said Humpty Dumpty, "which is to be master—that's all."

Alice was too much puzzled to say anything; so after a minute Humpty Dumpty began again. "They've a temper, some of them—particularly verbs: they're the proudest—adjectives you can do anything with, but not verbs—however, *I* can manage the whole lot of them! Impenetrability! That's what *I* say!"

"Would you tell me please," said Alice, "what that means?"

"Now you talk like a reasonable child," said Humpty Dumpty, looking very much pleased. "I meant by "impenetrability' that we've had enough of that subject, and it would be just as well if you'd mention what you mean to do next, as I suppose you don't mean to stop here all the rest of your life."

"That's a great deal to make one word mean," Alice said in a thoughtful tone.

"When I make a word do a lot of work like that," said Humpty Dumpty, "I always pay it extra."

The English language is the greatest single tool of man's long history. No writer could hope to know ten percent of what it holds, but if he does know some fraction of it well, that fraction will be all he needs for the writing of anything he is capable of thinking. The core of our language is the verb, the word that denotes an action, whether transitive, intransitive, or reflexive. The vigor and precision of a nonfiction passage can almost be gauged by the proportion of verbal-force words it contains. Passive verb forms often signal authorial hedging or limpness of thinking. Adverbs are another indication of writing failure. Exactly the right verb can eliminate the need for the adjective. Forms of the verb "to be" are to be avoided unless used for special emphasis (as I just did). To be or not to be, that *is* the question. These often-resented precepts are part of a technique for transmitting meanings from one human mind to another, and if flouting or bypassing them destroys the message, nothing has been accomplished. The age-old question of whether language is more important than content is actually unreal. A writer's language has to work on the reader.

Let us see how this is accomplished by looking at a number of examples. The first is from page one of Henry Adams's *Mont-Saint-Michel and Chartres:*

> The Archangel loved Heights. Standing on the summit of the tower that crowned his church, wings upspread, sword uplifted, the devil crawling beneath, and the cock, symbol of eternal vigilance, perched on his mailed foot, Saint Michael held a place of his own in heaven and on earth which seems, in the eleventh century, to leave hardly room for the Virgin of the Crypt at Chartres, still less for the Beau Christ of the thirteenth century at Amiens. The Archangel stands for Church and State, and both militant. He is the conqueror of Satan, the mightiest of all created spirits, the nearest to God. His place was where the danger was greatest; therefore you find him here.

Notice the extraordinary achievement of those first lines. They are instantly interesting. They are directly and vividly pictorial. They foreshadow the excitement of a dangerous age and a militant one. They span, as easily as a hawk turns in air, the three great accomplishments of French Gothic from the eleventh to the thirteenth century, and in doing so declare the theme of the book: a past of three centuries of French history expressed in its architecture. They promise change in that third of a millenium: "seems . . . to leave hardly room . . ." on to "still less for the Beau Christ. . . ." They move from a general past and effortlessly into a permanent present: "therefore you find him here." Notice the percentage of verbs or verbal-force words. Notice also that what is to come in the entire book has already been promised to the reader. *And* the style and tone of voice has been cleared and established.

And now another New England voice, almost contemporary with Adams, and very different: the voice of Captain Joshua Slocum. Here is the first paragraph of his book, *Sailing Alone Around the World*. I quote from *The Voyages of Joshua Slocum* by Walter Magnes Teller.

In the fair land of Nova Scotia, a maritime province, there is a ridge called North Mountain, overlooking the Bay of Fundy on one side and the fertile Annapolis valley on the other. On the northern slope of the range grows the hardy spruce-tree, well adapted for ship-timbers, of which many vessels of all classes have been built. The people of this coast, hardy, robust, and strong, are disposed to compete in the world's commerce, and it is nothing against the master mariner if the birthplace mentioned on his certificate be Nova Scotia. I was born in a cold spot, on coldest North Mountain, on a cold February 20, though I am a citizen of the United States—a naturalized Yankee, if it may be said that Nova Scotians are not Yankees in the truest sense of the word. On both sides my family were sailors; and if any Slocum should be found not seafaring, he will show at least an inclination to whittle models of boats and contemplate voyages. My father was the sort of man who, if wrecked on a desolate island, would find his way home, if he had a jackknife and could find a tree. He was a good judge of a boat, but the old clay farm which some calamity made his was an anchor to him. He was not afraid of a capful of wind, and he never took a back seat at a camp-meeting or a good, old-fashioned revival.

The Nonfiction Writer

Joshua Slocum was never to be able to swallow the anchor and settle into the land, even the temptingly fertile Annapolis valley, nor yet to endure the death-in-life to which his father had condemned himself. The first man to sail alone around the world refused to stop being a sea captain when the world had no longer need of master mariners of sail, and he built—or rebuilt—with his own hands and out of wood he chose himself, his last, his smallest, and his greatest command. He says the most of it in that opening paragraph, right down to the global nature of his finest achievement: "The people of this coast . . . are disposed to compete in the world's commerce. . . ." Notice the foreshadowing of the shipbuilding. Notice the pride and the solitariness. In twenty lines there are some thirty verbal words.

A third New England voice, a scholar's and a man's. Samuel Eliot Morison begins his book, *The European Discovery of America,* as follows:

> The European discovery of America flows from two impulses. One, lasting over two thousand years and never attained, is the quest for some "land of pure delight where saints immortal reign"; where (in the words of Isaac Watts's hymn) "everlasting spring abides, and never fading flowers." The other impulse, springing into life in the thirteenth century, was the search for a sea route to "The Indies," as China, Japan, Indonesia, and India were then collectively called. This search attained success with the voyages of Columbus and Cabot—who (by the greatest serendipity of history) discovered America instead of reaching the Indies—and with the voyage of Magellan which finally did reach the Indies and returned around the world.

In eleven lines of text there are more than twenty verbs or words of verbal force. Notice the establishment of time-scale and time, or geographical range, and also the germ of the greatest historical pressures, which occasioned the subject matters of the book. The first section to follow the opening deals with the religious pressures and includes an account of St. Brendan's voyages in search of the Promised Land, so the Watts's quote is felicitous. The yoking of Columbus with Cabot is deliberate and foreshadows one of the finest sections of the book. Again the reader cannot mistake the nature of the writing mind that is communicating with him. Firm, masculine, and assured—a sailor-man writing about sailors—it is also the voice of an historically and culturally sophisticated mind. And it is clearly the voice of a great teacher.

The last example is from an author who was a friend of mine and a onetime Bread Loaf Conference member and staff member, Catherine Drinker Bowen. The book is *Family Portrait,* published in 1970. Here she is on the first page of her first chapter, which she has entitled "Prelude to Bethlehem. A Dominance of Males." You don't have to read any further to know that you are in the company of a genuinely liberated mind and spirit. And a sense of humor.

When my sister Ernesta heard we were going to move to Bethlehem, Pennsylvania, she sat up in the cherry tree and cried for three days. My father had been named president of Lehigh University. I was eight and Ernesta thirteen, her life already established in suburban Philadelphia—her friends and her hopes and what I afterward learned were her ambitions. At this time, 1905, we lived on the campus of Haverford College, twenty minutes from town by the Paoli Local, on the Pennsylvania Railroad's main line to Pittsburgh. My parents still used the old phrase, they were "going to town on the cars."

There are seventeen words of verbal force in those eleven short lines. Notice the felicity of choosing a moment of change for the start of the book. Notice the density of that first sentence: the reader learns where the family is going to move—the "Bethlehem" of the title thus instantly becoming that less exotic one in Pennsylvania—and begins to learn something about Ernesta, that overacting sister in the cherry tree, who will later emerge as the willful and acknowledged beauty of the family. No word in that brief paragraph is superfluous and all of them combine to lure the reader back into the earlier world of a family securely rooted in suburban Philadelphia well before the turn of the century: "My parents still used the old phrase. . . ." And into something else as well: a sense that this particular portrait of a family will be no ordinary one.

Language aside, a book is something more than a random collection of words inked on paper. For one thing, the physical object tells the reader that. It has a shape like a sort of box with a place where you open it and a place where you close it. Usually, it has other architectural features as well—a name on its portal of entrance, a contents list like a directory board, and so on. But there is another shape, a structure that grows out of the writing process itself. *The writing process, properly conducted, is a process of selection.*

Any subject is a big and intricate one when fully explored. The nonfiction writer selects from the totality of his knowledge and his intention, as they reside in his mind, those elements that contribute most to his communication with the reader. Necessarily he selects them in sequences, sometimes enormously complicated ones, and equally necessarily he lays them out in an apparently or ostensibly simple sequence from page one to the end. These points are just as true for the article as for the book. Obviously they also apply to the chapters or sections of even the longest book. A chapter is only an incomplete or dependent article. All chapters depend on what has preceded them, except of course the first, and all chapters also presuppose what is to follow. Except of course the last.

So far as the reader is concerned all books progress from alpha to omega. The order in which they are read is the order in which they are experienced, though we all know how even a nonstudious reader will on occasion skip back to an earlier passage or forward to an anticipated and foreshadowed one. This reading order is not necessarily the order of the writing, and very often the beginning is among the last pages of the book to be written or rewritten. There are sound reasons for this. The beginning carries all the seeds.

If a book has a beginning, it also has an end. Nonfiction develops by increment, builds on its own material, and ends when its material has been completely exploited. If the book fulfills its contract with the reader, the end will complete the book by fulfilling the promises it made at the start. And if the people who read that book feel continuously that they are being added to and believe, at the end, that there is more to them than there was before, the work of nonfiction has succeeded. The same can be said of fiction as well. In both cases, the contract between writer and reader has been kept.